DUNAMIS
MADE SIMPLE

DUNAMIS MADE SIMPLE

© 2024 Patricia King Enterprises

All Rights Reserved. No part of this publication may be reproduced, stored in a retrieval system or transmitted in any form or by any means – electronic, mechanical, photocopy, recording or any other – without the prior written permission of the author.

Unless otherwise identified, Scripture quotations are taken from the New King James Version®. Copyright© 1982 by Thomas Nelson. Used by permission. All rights reserved.

Scripture quotations marked (NASB) are from the NEW AMERICAN STANDARD BIBLE®, copyright© 1960, 1962, 1963, 1968, 1971, 1972, 1973, 1975, 1977, 1995 by The Lockman Foundation. Used by permission. Scriptures quotations marked NASB1995 are taken from the NEW AMERICAN STANDARD BIBLE® 1995 revision.

Scripture quotations marked (AMPC) are taken from the Amplified Bible, Classic Edition, copyright© 1954, 1958, 1962, 1964, 1965, 1987 by The Lockman Foundation.

Scripture quotations marked (TPT) are from The Passion Translation®. Copyright© 2017, 2018, 2020 by Passion & Fire Ministries, Inc. Used by permission. All rights reserved.

Scripture quotations marked (NLT) are taken from the Holy Bible, New Living Translation, copyright© 1996, 2004, 2015 by Tyndale House Foundation. Used by permission of Tyndale House Publishers, Inc.

Scripture quotations marked (KJV) are taken from King James Version, public domain.

Scripture quotations marked (MSG) are taken from The Message, Copyright© 1993, 2002, 2018 by Eugene H. Peterson.

Scripture quotation marked (ERV) is taken from the Easy-to-Read Version, copyright © 2006 by Bible League International.

ISBN: 978-1-62166-550-2

Patricia King Enterprises

PATRICIAKING.COM

DUNAMIS
MADE **SIMPLE**

*A Guide to
Receiving and Activating
the Power of God*

PATRICIA KING

FOREWORD BY ROBERT HOTCHKIN

Dedicated to Holy Spirit

Thank You, Holy Spirit, for Your love, support, and unfailing commitment to those who believe.

"But you shall receive power
when the Holy Spirit has come upon you;
and you shall be witnesses to Me in Jerusalem,
and in all Judea and Samaria,
and to the end of the earth."

Acts 1:8

"The Holy Spirit's power is unlike any other in the world.
Only the power of the Holy Spirit can transform us, relieve our guilt, and heal our souls."

- Michael Youssef

Table of Contents

Foreword by Robert Hotchkin ... 11
We Need More Power!

Prophecy through Patricia King ... 17
Dunamis Outpouring in the Last Days

Chapter 1 ~ First Things First ... 21

Chapter 2 ~ The Greater Works ... 33

Chapter 3 ~ Receiving Dunamis ... 45

Chapter 4 ~ The Three-Strand Conduit ... 57

Chapter 5 ~ Miracle-Working Dunamis ... 71

Chapter 6 ~ Virtue-Producing Dunamis ... 89

Chapter 7 ~ Exponential Dunamis ... 101

Chapter 8 ~ Warfare Dunamis ... 113

Chapter 9 ~ Wealth-Creating Dunamis ... 135

Chapter 10 ~ You and Dunamis ... 155

Foreword

WE NEED MORE POWER!

by Robert Hotchkin

Throughout church history, God has had a very clear strategy to make us more effective in the sharing of the gospel. Power!

When Phillip went to Samaria in Acts 8:6, it says the crowds paid attention to the words Phillip spoke because of the power that he moved in.

The Apostle Paul was effective for the gospel everywhere he went. A big part of the reason for that was the notable and remarkable miracles that he worked along the way (see Acts 19).

The gospel is meant to be shared in word AND power (see 1 Corinthians 2:4), which is why Jesus tells us in Matthew 10:7-8 to go and declare that the Kingdom of Heaven is at hand. However, He is very clear that we are not only to tell people about the Kingdom of God, but we're also to show them displays of its power by healing the sick, raising the dead, casting out demons, and more.

Power Preaches

I remember as a new Christian being invited to be a part of a miracle crusade outside of Nazret, Ethiopia.

I didn't know much back then, other than Jesus was my Savior, and His Word was true. So when I read in Matthew 10:1 that Jesus gave His disciples the power and authority to heal every kind of disease, I started looking for opportunities to pray for the sick and see them healed by the power of Jesus. Before I knew it, I was in a field in eastern Africa with thousands of Ethiopians. As we prayed for them, we saw blind eyes opened, deaf ears opened, tumors disappear, the lame walk, the oppressed and demonized set free, and more. It was awesome!

My favorite testimony from those ten days was when a five-year-old boy, who had been deaf his entire life, came to the meetings (his big brother had walked with him from their village). In the name of Jesus, that boy's ears "popped" open and he could suddenly hear. The next day, his entire village showed up to be saved. Not because of a good message, but because the deaf-ear-opening power of Jesus declared to them that He was real and that He was God!

A Pure and Powerful Church

One of the things Jesus has promised us and paid for is the ability to be a church filled with POWER.

WE NEED MORE POWER

We are meant to move in power.

YOU are meant to move in power.

And here is a key – you already have it! While yes, we need "more" power, it's not really that we need to get more power. That would imply that God is withholding some of His power from us, which is contrary to what He tells us throughout the New Testament (e.g., Ephesians, 1:3, 22-23; 2 Peter 1:3; John 14:12, etc.).

What we need are more displays of the power that we already have. So what we're going after isn't more power so much as more insight into how we can see greater and more consistent manifestations of the dunamis power of God that we've already been given by the indwelling of His Holy Spirit.

I think one of the main keys to this is very simple. While it is absolutely the Spirit of God who fills us, overflows us, and reaches through us to heal, deliver, and work miracles, He is not the healing Spirit of God. Or the delivering Spirit of God. Or the miraculous spirit of God. Or even the powerful Spirit of God. He is the HOLY Spirit of God.

Has the modern church missed a very simple key to seeing more of the power of His HOLY Spirit in our lives? What if we were as willing to embrace His holiness as we are to move in His power? Perhaps if we more fully respond to His invitation to "be holy for I am holy" (1 Peter 1:15-16), we will see even more manifestations of His Holy Spirit power. Not because we are earning more power by working at being holy, but because we are choosing to be even fuller expressions and embodiments of who we truly are in Christ so that even more of what we already have manifests—in POWER!!

That's why I am so excited for you and so many other believers to get their hands (and minds and hearts) on this wonderful book by my dear friend Patricia King.

I can think of no one better to help guide us into a fuller understanding AND manifestation of the DUNAMIS power of the Holy Spirit than Patricia. For the twenty-plus years I have known her, she has been as committed to Kingdom values as much as Kingdom power. She has been as committed to righteousness and love as she has been to the supernatural and miracles. She has been as committed to the fruits of the Holy Spirit as she has been to the gifts of the Holy Spirit.

Thank you, Patricia, for *Dunamis Made Simple*. Thank you for helping us all step into more, greater, and more consistent displays of DUNAMIS power in all its fullness. And all to the glory of our Jesus who deserves a church that walks in His PURITY and POWER!!

Robert Hotchkin
Robert Hotchkin Ministries
Men on the Frontlines
Supernatural Mentoring Series
roberthotchkin.com

What Is Dunamis?

The word "power" in many New Testament verses is derived from the Greek word, *dynamis*, and is pronounced *"doo – nam – is"* (DUNAMIS). In this book, DUNAMIS is the word I use to refer to God's power. It means "inherent power, power residing in a thing by virtue of its nature, or which a person or thing exerts and puts forth." Dunamis includes:

1. The power to perform miracles
2. Moral power and excellence of soul
3. Power and resources that arise from numbers
4. Power consisting in or resting upon armies, forces, hosts
5. The power and influence which belong to riches and wealth

What Is Dunamis?

–Prophecy–

DUNAMIS OUTPOURING IN THE LAST DAYS

Through Patricia King

December 6, 2023

The last days will be challenging and treacherous times for those who do not know Me or cleave to Me, says the Lord. People will turn to evil, and they will thirst for blood. Many hearts will purpose to stand against Me and will attempt to overthrow My Kingdom and My righteousness. They will choose rebellion rather than obedience to My ways. They will choose pride instead of humility and hate rather than love.

They will give themselves to lawlessness rather than to virtue and integrity. Many who once had strong faith in Me will choose to believe the doctrine of demons and will compromise and twist My word and My ways, for their hearts will harden and their love will grow cold. They have chosen to obey their own carnal inclinations rather than My truth. They follow the pathways of their own determinations rather than choosing to be led by My Spirit.

The Righteous Remnant Arises

Even now the night is far spent, says the Lord, but I have raised up a righteous remnant whom I will clothe with My holy *dunamis power*, and I will establish them in My authority that is above all other rule and dominion. The last days will indeed be treacherous, oppressive, and filled with difficult times for those who walk contrary to My dominion, but the last days will be truly glorious for those who choose Me.

Watch and see what I will do through those I anoint with wisdom and great power in these days. The latter glory of the house will truly be greater than the former, and those who surrender to Me will be lavished with grace, peace, and blessing. You will watch Me raise up consecrated vessels filled with My power who will do exploits in My name and for My honor alone. Even now, My eyes are moving to and fro throughout the Earth, searching for those whose hearts are completely Mine so that I may show Myself strong on their behalf.

Bloodshed, Shakings, Wars, Assaults

There will be bloodshed, there will be shakings, there will be wars and rumors of wars. There will be violence in the streets and surprise assaults, but I have overcome it all. My power has, and will, conquer all the power and works of the enemy.

When you see the shakings, do not fear, for I have not given you a spirit of fear but of love, power, and a sound mind. Remember that you are Mine, and I will hold you close to My heart. Remember all the promises I have declared to you in My Word, for they have all been given to you through the eternal, unbreakable covenant I accomplished for you on the cross.

Do not fear the coming persecution against My righteousness. What can man do to you when I am holding you in My grip? You are blessed when you are persecuted for My purposes. Do not fear or lose your confidence. Your confidence in Me offers a great recompense of reward.

You are not on the defense, hiding from the battle that is raging. No! You are called to aggressively move the Kingdom forward in these days, and you will. Simply give Me your "yes." You will move mountains and obstacles, you will heal the sick, set the oppressed free, and proclaim freedom to prisoners. You will call dry bones to life, raise the dead, and cleanse the defiled. You will possess and occupy. You will pursue, overtake, and recover all.

You Are Invited

You are invited to be a powerful, chosen one, called by My name among many others who will come forth from their prayer closet manifesting great power and miracles. It is time to rejoice in the victories to come. It is time to arise and shine.

In the midst of the darkness, My light will bring illumination and exposure. My glory will be made manifest. My grace will increase, and a great harvest of souls will come into the Kingdom for such a time as this.

There will be two tracks in this day—Mine and the enemy's. Choose which track you will run on. My "dunamis power" is available to you in this critical hour. My people need My power. Pursue Me. Be filled. Saturate.

Confirming Scriptures

2 Timothy 3:1-5
Haggai 2:6-9
2 Chronicles 16:9
2 Timothy 1:7
Luke 24:49
Acts 1:8
Matthew 5:10-12
Isaiah 60
Hebrews 10:35–36
1 Samuel 30:1-8

Chapter 1

FIRST THINGS FIRST

The Not-So-Mighty Woodpecker

While hiking through a forest, a novice backpacker noticed a woodpecker fervently pecking the trunk of a tree. He took out his binoculars and zoomed in for a close-up view of this marvelous creature at work. Impressive indeed! Due to his complete focus on the woodpecker, he failed to notice a lightning bolt hit the top of the tree, splitting it right down its center. The hiker was filled with amazement as he gazed upon this mighty display of power coming from such a small bird. With excitement and awe, he shouted at the top of his lungs, "Wow, what a beak!"

This story concluded with a ridiculous assumption, so you are probably chuckling right now. Unfortunately, we see this misguided response regularly, regarding the manifestation of power. Throughout mankind's history, full credit and honor have been given to mere men and women who created inventions sourced by power. Sadly, even in the church, we find accolades directed toward those who minister the anointing, gifts of the Holy Spirit, and the miracle works of God with barely even a mention of the One who is the source of such grace and supernatural might.

God, the Source of Power

All power is sourced in God. Without God, power would not be present. If you cut off the source, you cut off the power. A while back, our electrical power went out in our home. As a result, nothing that functioned by power worked—not the lights, electrical outlets, garbage disposal, oven, dishwasher, coffee maker, fridge, or television. And when the battery charge wore off, even our computers and cell phones failed to function. Anything and everything connected to power failed to perform. The reason? Part of the electrical grid that supplied power for the city had been compromised. As a result of the source being hit, an entire part of the city lost its power. Every home in the affected area lacked power. No traffic lights in the area worked. No power!

Imagine, for a moment, God leaving planet Earth completely, taking His power with Him, and settling in a new galaxy somewhere else. The arrogant say, "We don't need God. We have our own beliefs—our own ways. We have science. We have technology. Man created the lightbulb, not God. Man created high-powered nuclear weapons, not God." What arrogance! Psalm 14:1 declares that the fool believes in his heart, "There is no God." When the source is removed, power is eliminated. It is only by the mercy of God that we have power to enjoy and utilize, as He can withdraw it at any time.

Make no mistake, all power is sourced in God. He is the creator of Power.

FIRST THINGS FIRST

> "God has spoken once,
> Twice I have heard this:
> That **power** *belongs* **to God.**"
> –*Psalm 62:11*

> "You are worthy, O Lord,
> To receive glory and honor and **power;**
> for You created all things,
> And by Your will they exist and were created."
> –*Revelation 4:11*

> "And He Himself existed *and* is before all things,
> and **in Him all things hold together.**
> [His is the controlling, cohesive force of the universe.]"
> –*Colossians 1:17 (AMP)*

All Honor Belongs to God

Because all power is sourced in God, it is vital that He receives the honor for the righteous fruit it produces. When we demand recognition or personally desire the accolades of our fellow humans for demonstrating God's anointing, power, and works, we step into ludicrous self-idolatry. This is exactly what Lucifer did when he served God as a ministering angel. When he demanded the honor, he was cast out, and we know how that worked out for him. Let his nature and choices be far from us!

If we are going to be used by God to manifest His great power and glory in these coming days, we must acknowledge Him as the source and not make prideful claims to exalt ourselves.

All of heaven constantly acknowledges all that God is and all that He does; He is honored and worshipped. Our only appropriate and holy response is to also grant Him the honor He deserves on Earth. Oh, may it be on Earth as it is in heaven!

> Then I looked, and I heard the voice of many angels around the throne, the living creatures, and the elders; and the number of them was ten thousand times ten thousand, and thousands of thousands, saying with a loud voice:
>
> "Worthy is the Lamb who was slain To receive power and riches and wisdom, And strength and honor and glory and blessing!"
>
> And every creature which is in heaven and on the earth and under the earth and such as are in the sea, and all that are in them, I heard saying:
>
> "Blessing and honor and glory and power be to Him who sits on the throne, and to the Lamb, forever and ever!"
>
> –Revelation 5:11-13

I have seen many rise to great recognition because they've manifested God's power. Unfortunately, I have also seen too many fall as a result of being self-enamored when they ministered such power. Several of them were snared by multiple temptations in diverse areas, but the primary root was pride.

What do you do when you are honored by others?

The Lord is worthy to receive ALL honor. This is appropriate, and yet you are His co-laborer in releasing His power and glory in the Earth. His plan is to reveal His glory through you;

therefore, you must be willing to partner with Him. The source of power is in Him, but the minister of His power is you. When someone is blessed by your ministry and they proceed to give you honor, receive it graciously, then give it to the Lord in worship and thanksgiving.

With joy receive the honor and then, in turn, honor Him with the honor you were given. Joyfully receive, and then joyfully cast your crowns at His feet.

> "Greatness, power, glory, victory, and honor belong to You, because everything in heaven and on earth belongs to You! The kingdom belongs to You, Lord! You are the head, the ruler over everything." – *1 Chronicles 29:11 (ERV)*

In this book, I will teach you how to receive and minister all five aspects of God's dunamis power, but settle in your heart, now and for all time, that all the power is sourced in God. He deserves your wholehearted participation in releasing it and the honor as the source of it.

"If you look up into His face and say, 'Yes, Lord, whatever it costs,' at that moment He'll flood your Life with His presence and power."

- Alan Redpath

For Good or for Evil

Every gift and enablement comes from God but can be utilized for good or for evil. Even though power is sourced in God, mankind can use it for good or evil. We choose how and when we use our gifts and God-given skills.

> "Do not be deceived, my beloved brethren.
> Every good gift and every perfect gift is from above,
> and comes down from the Father of lights,
> with whom there is no variation or shadow of turning."
> *–James 1:16-18*

Let's look at the verses that directly precede the above portion. They offer us an important warning concerning the good and perfect gifts that God gives. The gifts are perfect and flawless in origin but can be used for evil purposes. How? By giving in to temptation.

> Blessed is the man who endures temptation; for when he has been approved, he will receive the crown of life which the Lord has promised to those who love Him. Let no one say when he is tempted, "I am tempted by God"; for God cannot be tempted by evil, nor does He Himself tempt anyone. But each one is tempted when he is drawn away by his own desires and enticed. Then, when desire has conceived, it gives birth to sin; and sin, when it is full-grown, brings forth death. *–James 1:12-15*

Jesus taught us to pray:

"Lead us not into temptation but deliver us from evil: for thine is the kingdom, and the power, and the glory, forever. Amen" *–Matthew 6:13 (KJV)*

We often pass over this scripture lightly because we have become so familiar with it, but there was a valuable reason why Jesus used this directive to teach us to pray. The devil is roaming around like a roaring lion seeking someone to devour (1 Peter 5:8). He desires us to become self-focused and self-idolizing, following our own ways rather than God's. He unsuccessfully tempted Jesus in the wilderness. He will try to tempt you too.

A certain minister was empowered with a prophetic gift. He was very accurate. His gift became known and as a result, many came knocking on his door, desiring personal prophecies. He served them well with his gift, and God blessed him with increased revelation and favor.

His favor and fame grew, and he was invited to speak and prophesy at all kinds of venues—conferences, church meetings, business seminars, and government offices. When he noticed the grace of prophecy waning at some of his meetings, he began to fear that he would lose fame (and fortune), so… he cheated. I won't go into the details, but he received insight from sources that were not from God. Once you give into temptation, it will bring you into deeper and deeper deception. It doesn't go away. You become a slave to what you give yourself to and eventually, your sin will find you out. He was eventually caught in the very act.

Another minister was known for specific words of knowledge that amazed multitudes and drew crowds to his meetings. He was publicly exposed for wearing an earpiece with someone feeding him information. This level of deception did not happen overnight. He was a man with a true gift, authentic anointing, and he ministered in effective dunamis power, but he fell into temptation along the way, and it eventually destroyed his ministry and reputation.

Jesus taught us to take up our cross daily and follow Him. The cross is an instrument of death. If we die to selfish ambition, pride, and desire for fame, then power will not corrupt. If we choose to always humble ourselves and exalt and honor God, the source of all power, we will be kept from harm.

> "Only in the Cross of Christ will we receive power when we are powerless.
> We will find strength when we are weak.
> We will experience hope when our situation is hopeless.
> Only in the Cross is there peace for our troubled hearts."
>
> *- Michael Youssef*

Only One Way of Escape

If you are ever ensnared by temptation and sin, the only way to escape is to bring full disclosure and commit to full repentance. Often, when believers are caught in a transgression, they lie to cover it up or they just confess at a partial level. As a result, they never come free. The devil fully understands this dynamic and will keep the sin covered… until it's not!

I set a notification on my phone that beeps every hour on the hour. It is a reminder to pray, "Lead me not into temptation, and deliver me from the evil one and his snares." Never underestimate the power of carnal flesh. All of mankind fell because of one couple's transgression, even though they lived in a perfectly holy environment with a perfect and holy God. We never want to be "sin conscious" but rather should be focused on who we are in Christ as His righteousness. Whatever you focus on, you empower.

I do not want to empower sin in my life by focusing on it. That is why I pray with excitement, faith, and expectation when I pray Matthew 6:13—not from fear of being tempted and falling.

When we pray in faith, Jesus protects us from temptation and delivers us from the evil plots of the enemy. Because we pray, we stand. God is faithful.

> "Now unto Him that is able to keep you from falling, and to present you faultless before the presence of His glory with exceeding joy, to the only wise God our Savior, be glory and majesty, dominion and power, both now and ever. Amen." –Jude 1:24–25

"Grace is not simply leniency when we have sinned. Grace is the enabling gift of God not to sin. Grace is power, not just pardon."

- John Piper

Are You Ready?

Here is your "get ready" checklist as you begin your journey to receive and minister the dunamis power of God:

1. You believe that God alone is the source of all power.
2. You believe that as the source of all power, He deserves all the honor and the glory.
3. You are committed to ministering His power in humility with purity of motive and purpose.

ACTIVATE

1. Take time to worship God as the God of ALL power/dunamis. Exalt Him above all else in your life.
2. Invite the Holy Spirit to convict you of any selfish motive or pride, and repent. Receive forgiveness (1 John 1:9).
3. Meditate on the following scriptures and allow the Lord to speak to your heart through them. Journal any insights that come to you.

Hebrews 3:3

"For this One has been counted worthy of more glory than Moses, inasmuch as He who built the house has more honor than the house."

Exodus 9:11

"But indeed for this *purpose* I have raised you up, that I may show My power *in* you, and that My name may be declared in all the earth."

2 Chronicles 20:6

"O LORD God of our fathers, *are* You not God in heaven, and do You *not* rule over all the kingdoms of the nations, and in Your hand *is there not* power and might, so that no one is able to withstand You?"

2 Chronicles 29:12b

"In Your hand *is* power and might; In Your hand *it is* to make great and to give strength to all."

Pray the following prayer:

Heavenly Father, I desire to give You glory by ministering Your dunamis power. Grant me revelation and understanding on how to walk in the paths You have set before me. Empower me with Your grace, and fill me with humility and purity as I grow in relationship with You and manifest Your dunamis to those in need. Keep me from temptation and the snares of the evil one. In Jesus' name, AMEN.

DECREE

In Jesus' name I am clothed in humility, filled with love, faith, and purity and am empowered by dunamis. I am filled with the very nature of Jesus Christ and am a consecrated vessel, set apart for advancing the Kingdom of God under the anointing of the Holy Spirit.

Chapter 2

THE GREATER WORKS

Take a step back in time for a moment and imagine yourself traveling with Jesus, just like His early disciples did when He ministered on the Earth. Seriously! Can you imagine yourself in your mind's eye right beside Him as He raised Jairus' daughter from her death bed? Or consider when He calmed the raging sea and silenced the storm, or when He cast out a legion of devils from the demoniac. Imagine yourself right there with Him as He healed Bartimaeus of blindness, or when He cleansed lepers and made them whole, or when He healed ALL the sick and oppressed that came to Him (see Matthew 8:16). Who wouldn't want to experience Him during even one of those events? Perhaps you are thinking, "I wish I could have been a fly on the wall!"

His disciples lived with Jesus and daily witnessed His glorious, supernatural works. For His disciples, this was normal, everyday life.

Most of us would give up everything to live such a life and calling, and yet, Jesus boldly declared, "Most assuredly, I say to you, he who believes in Me, the works that I do he will do also;

and greater *works* than these he will do, because I go to My Father" (John 14:12).

Not only are we invited to watch Him at work, but He also says we will actually perform His works. In fact, He expects those who believe in Him to do the works. That's right—it is His expectation.

What could be greater than walking on water, feeding the five thousand with just a few loaves and some fish, stilling storms, calming the sea, healing all the sick and oppressed that came to you, raising the dead, and casting out devils?

The word "greater" in John 14:12 is derived from a Greek word, "meizon," meaning greater, larger, and stronger. He declared that the works His church would perform would be greater in number, strength, and influence than His.

Instead of only One working the miracles, there would be a body of believers all committed to manifesting His glory and power. His plan included Him dying on the cross and going to the Father. Consequently, His Spirit (the same Spirit that anointed Him with power and raised Him from the dead), would be given to all who believed so they would do the works that He did.

When you minister God's power (dunamis), you are fulfilling one of Christ's deepest dreams and longings. You are giving Him what He lived and died for—a body of believers who will manifest the Kingdom of heaven in the Earth as He did and even in greater ways.

Review carefully the following commissioning scriptures that confirm this:

THE GREATER WORKS

Mark 16:15-20

And He said to them, "Go into all the world and preach the Gospel to every creature. He who believes and is baptized will be saved; but he who does not believe will be condemned. And these signs will follow those who believe: In My name they will cast out demons; they will speak with new tongues; they will take up serpents; and if they drink anything deadly, it will by no means hurt them; they will lay hands on the sick, and they will recover." So then, after the Lord had spoken to them, He was received up into heaven, and sat down at the right hand of God. And they went out and preached everywhere, the Lord working with *them* and confirming the word through the accompanying signs. Amen.

Matthew 10:7–8

"And as you go, preach, saying, 'The kingdom of heaven is at hand.' Heal the sick, cleanse the lepers, raise the dead, cast out demons. Freely you have received, freely give."

Luke 10:2–3,9,17-19

Then He said to them, "The harvest truly is great, but the laborers are few; therefore pray the Lord of the harvest to send out laborers into His harvest. Go your way; behold, I send you out as lambs among wolves... Whatever city you enter... heal the sick there, and say to them, 'The kingdom of God has come near to you."

Then the seventy returned with joy, saying, "Lord, even the demons are subject to us in Your name." And He said to them, "I saw Satan fall like lightning from heaven.

Behold, I give you the authority to trample on serpents and scorpions, and over all the power of the enemy, and nothing shall by any means hurt you."

The Early Church

When you read the book of Acts, can you imagine yourself right there with the disciples as they proclaim the gospel of the Kingdom, manifesting the powerful miracle works of Jesus? Can you see yourself at Gate Beautiful when the lame beggar, who had never walked in his life, was healed, letting everyone know about it as he leapt around, loudly praising God? (See Acts 3:2-10.)

Or perhaps you can find yourself praising the Lord while shackled with chains in the vile inner prison with Paul and Silas because you took a stand for Jesus. Suddenly the Lord shows up with an earthquake that sets all the prisoners free. Yes, all the prison doors are opened. The jailer is terrified, but hey, revival breaks out, and the jailer and his family are saved in the midst of it all! (See Acts 16:22-34.)

In Ephesus, Paul was working so many extraordinary miracles that folks were bringing aprons and handkerchiefs for him to touch. As a result, people were healed and delivered from demons when the anointed cloths touched them (see Acts 19:11-12). What a transference of power! Can you see yourself in that story?

God wrote the book for YOU! He wants you to see yourself with Him in every story… in every account. The power-filled apostles of the early church were prototypes for believers throughout all the ages. What Jesus did through them, He will do through you … and even greater!

The Return of Jesus

Scripture makes it clear that Jesus is returning for His church. We don't know when, but we know for sure He is not returning for a church that is powerless and hiding out in caves, eating tribulation food. He is coming back for a glorious church—not a wimpy, powerless church!"

"That He might present her to Himself a glorious church…"
–*Ephesians 5:27a*

Revelation 19:7 states that His bride "…has made herself ready." Church, it is time to prepare and no longer delay. In the parable of the ten virgins (Matthew 25:1-13), we discover a valuable warning from the Lord. All ten were virgins. All ten knew the bridegroom was coming. All ten even had lamps, but only five had enough oil.

Oil in the Scripture often refers to the anointing of the Holy Spirit. We need the Holy Spirit's power today like never before. It is time to prepare in His presence and to receive fresh anointing and power. Jesus is coming back for a church that represents Him in the way He modeled in the Gospels and in the book of Acts—but even in greater ways and measures!

The Good News

The church is now about two thousand years old and has grown in numbers since the upper room outpouring of the

Spirit. Some missiologists estimate that more believers are alive on Earth today than there are in heaven. If their calculations are accurate, then more have been saved and are populating the Earth in this generation than the sum of all who have been saved and passed on to glory over the last two thousand years. That is mind-boggling.

Currently there are about 2.5 billion who profess the Christian faith in a world that is populated with around eight billion people. That is a few more believers than the upper room held when the church was born on Pentecost following Christ's ascension! According to current statistics, Christianity is by far the largest faith group in the world today.

Although there is room for the church to grow in numbers and in the demonstration of supernatural power and divine visitation, we are truly seeing expansion and increase in this hour. Haggai prophesied that the latter glory of the house would be greater than the former (see Haggai 2:9). We have a lot to look forward to.

I remember back in the early 1980s, when I taught classes on the gifts of the Holy Spirit, very few had experienced angelic visitation, supernatural healings in their bodies, deliverance from demons, or the receiving of divine revelation and prophetic insights. When I asked a class of perhaps one hundred students, three or four individuals testified to experiencing any of these things. Today, however, in the same size of class, over eighty percent will testify to personal experiences in these areas. The manifestations of supernatural power and divine encounters are on the increase, and we as believers can be positioned to both receive and activate.

The Coming Move: Presence, Purity, and Power

I personally have a strong conviction and prophetic witness that the greatest move of the Spirit in all biblical and church history awaits us. The coming move will be marked by God's presence, purity, and power—not just one of those characteristics will be manifest but ALL of them! This outpouring will not be confined to one geographical area or any specific church affiliation, rather, it will spread globally and saturate all who are hungry, regardless of what church they attend. Visitations and encounters in God's presence and with angelic hosts will increase, the fire of God and the Spirit of the fear of the Lord will purify the church, and His power with all the Holy Spirit's gifts and signs and wonders will be manifested beyond comprehension.

The Kingdom of God Is a Kingdom of Power

Let's look at some scriptures that might help you identify the will of God concerning your representation of Him and His Kingdom in the world you inhabit.

1 Corinthians 4:20 (NASB)

"For the kingdom of God does not consist in words but in **power**."

Question: Do you just talk about God, or do you manifest His power?

Ephesians 3:20 (NASB)

"Now to Him who is able to do far more abundantly beyond all that we ask or think, according to the **power** that works within us."

Question: Are you seeing God regularly move in your life in ways that far exceed all your expectations?

Colossians 1:29 (NASB)

"For this purpose also I labor, striving according to His **power,** which **mightily** works within me."

Question: Do you find yourself passionately pursuing and effectively activating the release of His power that resides in you?

We are responsible to give Jesus what He died for. He is calling His church to manifest HIM in fullness and not just fulfil religious duties or outward expectations. Jesus said, "As the Father has sent Me, so also I send you" (John 20:21). Does His church look and act like Him? Does His church love like Him? Does His church talk like Him? Does His church move in power like Him?

Now, let's get personal and ask the same questions of ourselves as valuable members of His global ecclesia (church). Do **I** look and act like Jesus? Do **I** love like Him? Do **I** talk like Him? Do **I** move in power like Him?

You might be feeling a big "ouch" after pondering those questions—I did! But the Lord never condemns—He convicts and invites. If you feel convicted, you are also invited to receive His mercy, grace, and power. He has chosen you to fill the Earth with all that He is and all that He does! That's right: **You** are called and chosen to manifest His nature, Kingdom, and power (dunamis)!

> "You cannot do God's work without God's power."
>
> *- John R. Rice*

What is Dunamis?

According to *Strong's Concordance of the New Testament*, the word that is used for power in most cases is a Greek word, "dynamis" (pronounced, "doo-nam-is" – DUNAMIS).

It means, inherent power, power residing in a thing by virtue of its nature, or which a person or thing exerts and puts forth and includes:

1. The power for performing miracles.
2. Moral power and excellence of soul.
3. The power and resources arising from numbers.
4. Power consisting in or resting upon armies, forces, hosts.
5. The power and influence which belong to riches and wealth.

Throughout this book, we will look at each of these aspects of His divine "dunamis" (similar references to the word, "power" in the Old Testament will also be used). You will discover how you can position yourself to receive and activate each one. Although this is a divine invitation, it is not really an option. If we are going to rightly represent Jesus in the world today, we must manifest

His dunamis. Are you willing to give Him your "yes" to the invitation? Are you ready to begin the glorious journey with the God of all dunamis? He is ready and waiting for you.

> "God's mighty power comes when God's people learn to walk with God."
>
> *- Jack Hyles*

ACTIVATE

1. Take some time to invite the Holy Spirit to search your heart concerning anything that would keep you from moving in more of His power. As you wait on Him, what thoughts come to you? Perhaps thoughts of unworthiness and inadequacy? Lack of hunger? Lack of understanding?

2. If anything comes to mind, receive forgiveness, and invite the Holy Spirit to help you overcome that area. He will. He is greater than anything you have and will ever face. There is no problem or obstacle too great for Him to overcome. He partners with you for success. He loves you!

3. Invite the Holy Spirit to cleanse your imagination, and then ask Him to help you dream, envision, and imagine what it would be like to walk with Jesus when He was in the Earth.

4. Imagine yourself with Him as He performed miracles. Journal what you see.

DECREE

I fulfill Christ's longing for a people who will manifest the greater works of His Kingdom. He is able to do exceedingly abundantly above all I could ask or think, according to the power that works mightily within me. He grants me the desires of my heart and as a result, I manifest His power and glory. I am filled with His Spirit and power.

Chapter 3

RECEIVING DUNAMIS

Jesus came to the Earth fully "man" even though He was and always will be fully God (see Philippians 2:6-8). When we observe the life and ministry of Jesus, we see who we are created to be, for when we receive Christ into our hearts, we carry His very nature and ministry within us. Because He lives within us by His Spirit, we can potentially think like Him, talk like Him, and act like Him.

Jesus was anointed with the Holy Spirit and dunamis.

"God anointed Jesus of Nazareth with the Holy Spirit and with **power**, who went about **doing good** and **healing all who were oppressed by the devil, for God was with Him**."
–Acts 10:38.

Let's apply Acts 10:38 to you, personally. In the same way Jesus was anointed, you are anointed. Jesus has sent you in the same way the Father sent Him (John 20:2).

1. **Jesus was anointed with the Holy Spirit and power (DUNAMIS).**

   If Christ lives in you, you have access to everything He has. You have the same anointing of the Holy Spirit and DUNAMIS available to you. The anointing is what sets you apart for God's service. Anointing means: "to smear or rub with oil, i.e., (by implication) to consecrate to an office or religious service."[1] Jesus was smeared with the Holy Spirit and DUNAMIS. You can be too.

2. **Jesus went about doing good.**

   The words "doing good" in this verse mean "to bestow benefits upon."[2] The Holy Spirit and dunamis enabled Jesus to go about everywhere and bestow benefits upon those He met and interacted with. I wrote a small book titled *Blessed to Bless*, which unpacks for the reader the covenant of blessing we have been given in Christ and how God has purposed for us to be His benefactors—those who lavish others with blessing. You are empowered to be blessed and to be a blessing. Like Jesus, everywhere you go, you will bestow benefits because you are anointed with dunamis.

3. **He healed all who were oppressed by the devil.**

   Sickness and disease are indeed oppressive in nature—I'm sure you have never felt happy and free when sick or afflicted with disease. In Jesus' day, He healed all the sick who came to Him, attacked defilement and shame by cleansing the lepers, and overpowered death by ministering resurrection at funerals.

---

[1] *Strong's Concordance of the New Testament*
[2] *Strong's Concordance* – Acts 10:38

1 John 3:8 says that Jesus had a specific purpose in coming to Earth: to destroy the works of the evil one. Anything contrary to God's blessings are works of the evil one, and Jesus came to destroy those things that stand in our way. You are also empowered to heal and set free all who are oppressed by the devil. You will grow in confidence to do so as you examine the truth about YOU—His carrier and distributor of "dunamis power."

4. **God was with Him.**

Jesus was God, but He came to Earth as our Redeemer in the form of a man. He had to fulfill the eternal, unbreakable love-covenant of salvation, reconciliation, and blessing "for man" and "as a man." In other words, He could not use His inherent "Godness" to fulfill the covenant. He had to walk "as a man" and with God. The awesome triune God (Father, Son, and Spirit) was in complete united agreement with the plan. The Man Jesus was also named Immanuel which means "God with us" because God was with Him.

> "Behold, the virgin shall be with child, and bear a Son, and they shall call His name Immanuel," which is translated, 'God with us.'" –*Matthew 1:23*

Jesus promised to always be with you, and He gave you His very own Spirit to fill you, to be upon you, and to empower you. John 14:16-18 and John 16:5-15 reveal the promise of the Father to give the Holy Spirit to those who believe in Christ. The Holy Spirit will teach, lead, guide, strengthen, support, reveal, and disclose truth and promise to those to whom He is sent. That means YOU, if you believe in Christ as your personal Lord and

Savior. Jesus said He would be with you always even to the end of the age (Matthew 28:20).

Imagine yourself in Christ fulfilling Acts 10:38:

1. **You are smeared with the fresh oil of the Holy Spirit and dunamis.**

   You are completely filled and outwardly smeared with the anointing of the Holy Spirit and dunamis. You are fully set apart for God and His Kingdom purposes.

2. **You go about doing good.**

   You are a blessing everywhere you go. You have been granted power to bless and bestow benefits upon those you meet. There is no limit to the blessings that flow through you to others, and the more you bless, the more you are blessed in return. You are a blessing conduit and are known for your good works and acts of kindness. You are created and empowered to do good.

3. **You heal all who are oppressed of the devil.**

   You are filled with power to destroy the works of the evil one. When you see someone struggling with sickness, you minister healing. When you see someone oppressed by the devil, you bring freedom. You are filled with dunamis, and as a result, you work miracles, signs, and wonders.

4. **God is with you.**

   You are not alone. God is always with you, and you are always with Him. You are inseparable. Everywhere you go, He goes.

Whatever you do, He is there with you to lead and guide you into all truth.

You Shall Receive Dunamis

Dunamis power is available to every believer, but not every believer will walk in it. It is for those who pursue and receive. It is for YOU.

> "But you shall **receive** power (dunamis) when the Holy Spirit has come upon you; and you shall be witnesses to Me in Jerusalem, and in all Judea and Samaria, and to the end of the earth." –*Acts 1:8*

In Acts 1:8 we find three keys regarding Dunamis:

1. **Dunamis is activated when the Holy Spirit comes upon you.**

When you are born again, the Holy Spirit comes into your human spirit.

> "That which is born of the flesh is flesh, and that which is born of the Spirit is spirit." –*John 3:6*

When "born of the Spirit," you become a brand-new creation. Old things have passed away and all things become new (see 2 Corinthians 5:17).

In the Holy Spirit are His power, gifts, character, wisdom, and everything that pertains to Him. He came into your spirit when you asked Christ into your life by faith, and therefore His power, gifts, and wisdom are also in you.

Jesus promised His disciples in Acts 1:5 that they would be "baptized in the Holy Spirit." To baptize means to completely fill or to fully immerse. It is not "a little dab will do ya."

I was adding a vitamin fizzy to a bottle of water one day. I had carefully broken the vitamin tablet in small pieces so it could easily dissolve. I then added another one for good measure (if one gives results, then two will increase the results—right?). I put the lid on and shook the bottle to dissolve the tablets. I then took the cap off and it erupted. The fizzy tablets caused the water to bubble up and overflow. The bottle was soaked with "fizzy" and so were my hands and the floor around me. What was in the bottle came out with force.

That is how the baptism with the Holy Spirit works. He is already in you when you receive Christ as your Savior, but when you are baptized in the Spirit, He fills every part of your being and comes upon you. When He comes upon you, dunamis can manifest to the world around you.

Baptism in the Spirit is not a one-time encounter. You can be constantly and continually filled with the Holy Spirit (see Ephesians 5:18). Invite Him to fill you afresh right now and then believe that you are. Don't wait for a specific feeling or sensation—simply believe, intentionally receive, and call yourself filled. Jesus said, "Therefore I say to you, whatever things you ask when you pray, believe that you receive them, and you will have them" (Mark 11:24).

He didn't say, "When you pray and feel warm all over," or "When you pray and lightning bolts flash out of heaven and hit your body," or "When you pray and the angel appears." He said, "**When you pray, believe that you receive** ... and you shall have it." Faith is your connector to divine promises, not feelings or circumstances.

Be filled and closely acquainted with the Holy Spirit. He is amazing and He is with you, right now!

2. **Dunamis must be received.**

When I think of the word "receive," I sense that someone will come to me with something, and I simply receive it from them. The one who delivers the blessing does the work, and I sit back and receive. It is easy. In many ways, that is how we obtain all the blessings and promises of God. We "receive" them by faith.

However, the original word in the Greek for "receive' in Acts 1:8 does not indicate a passive receiving but an active pursuit. Acts 1:8 says, "You shall **receive** power..." The word "receive" is a key for unlocking and igniting the dunamis in you.

The root word in the Greek for "receive" is *lambano*. It means:
to take; to lay hold of; to seize; to take possession; to gain; to obtain, when taken is not let go, to apprehend.

Can you see the action and intentional, focused pursuit alluded to in those definitions?

A Fun and Powerful Prophetic Exercise

Sometimes I find it helpful to engage in a prophetic act when I am laying hold of a promise. I will meditate on the promise and get excited about receiving it. I then stand up, lift my arm high into the air above my head, and grab hold of the promise by faith. I hold it tightly and bring my hand down to my heart and "receive it" by faith into my life. I then say, "It's mine! I've got it!" Sometimes I will repeat that little exercise a few times until it really sinks in.

I realize that you might find my "prophetic action" a little strange for your liking, but do you realize that there is a powerful connection between your spirit, soul, and body? Your body performs the works that your soul chooses and is strengthened and empowered by your spirit. As the soul affects your body, so can your body influence your soul and the way you think and feel.

I heard a sports psychologist share a seminar about the powerful influence the physical body has upon the soul. She shared the example of professional athletes who are taught to hold several "victory poses" for a minimum of two minutes each before a game.

The psychologist had those attending the seminar test it. She first assigned us a victory pose—we were to reach our arms up high in a victory formation with our fingers extended and our feet firmly planted on the ground, spread the same distance apart as our extended arms. We held the pose for two minutes. I found the exercise to be very enlightening indeed. When I engaged in the victory pose, my thoughts turned positive and victorious, and I increased in focus and emotional determination the longer I posed. She gave us more poses, and when I engaged, I found my soul to be filled with refreshing positivity and victory-producing energy.

This exercise will help you focus on receiving dunamis if you care to give it a try. Meditate on the promise that Jesus gave you in Acts 1:8. Get excited about receiving dunamis.

Okay, now for the "pose"—come on, you can do it! Stand up, lift your arm high into the air above your head, as though you are reaching into heaven, and grab hold of dunamis by faith. Hold it tightly for a few moments, then bring your hand holding the promise down to your heart and "receive it" by faith into your body, soul, and spirit. Declare with bold confidence, "It's mine! I've got it!" What do you have? You have dunamis! By faith, you have received God's power.

Faith is internal reality and not just a casual belief in your mind. Work the promise by meditating on it, speaking it, and activating it until faith is produced ... and once faith is produced, work the promise some more by meditating on it, speaking it, and activating it! You position yourself to produce faith, and then your faith will produce the promise. (There will be more in-depth teaching on faith in the next chapter, but this will at least start your engine.)

Take a few moments and activate the promise of dunamis **again** right now if you'd like. You can use this little activation on any promise. Stand up, lift your arm high into the air above your head, and with your hand grab hold of the promise—by faith. Hold your hand tightly for a few moments and then bring it down and press it into your heart. Then declare with bold confidence, "It's mine! I've got it!"

The Holy Spirit's dunamis is mine! I have it! Dunamis fills me!

Do you have it yet? If not, what are you waiting for? Go get it.

3. **Dunamis empowers you to be His witness.**

Having dunamis in you is wonderful, but it can't just sit there inside of you. It needs to be activated so you can do the works of Jesus. You are called to be a witness—a proclaimer in word and deed of His existence and truth. Begin to activate His dunamis. Remember it is already in you. It is yours! You have it! Now exercise it! You release the dunamis of God that is within you by faith.

> Jesus said, "And as you go, preach, saying, 'The kingdom of heaven is at hand.' Heal the sick, cleanse the lepers, raise the dead, cast out demons. Freely you have received, freely give."
> – Matthew 10:7-8

> "The Holy Spirit is the gift of the Risen Christ. His anointing and empowering work is a baptism of love that gives power to make Jesus real to you and known to others."
>
> *- Winkie Pratney*

ACTIVATE

I have already given you a few activations, but here's another I think you will enjoy.

RECEIVING DUNAMIS

Jesus said,

"Behold, I send the promise of My Father upon you; but tarry in the city of Jerusalem until you are endued with power from on high." –*Luke 24:49*

The word tarry means to position in a sitting position, and Jerusalem means "set ye double peace." In other words, when we are looking to receive dunamis, we are not going to strive or get anxious. We are going to position ourselves in peace and intentionally receive the promise by faith.

The word endued in Luke 24:49 means: to sink into (clothing), put on, clothe oneself.[3] I love that image—being clothed with power. Now, let's use the same prophetic exercise as before while we meditate on this promise.

1. Sit and meditate on the promise of being clothed with power. Imagine yourself wearing a garment called dunamis.

2. Drink in His assurance and peace.

3. When you are ready to receive, stand up, stretch both arms over your head, grab your dunamis garment by faith and clothe yourself in it. Enjoy wearing it. Believe in the reality of being clothed with dunamis power.

4. With joy, decree, "It is mine! I have it! I am wearing dunamis!"

5. Now walk around enjoying your new garment and look for places and people where you can release dunamis.

---

3 *Strong's Concordance* – Greek endyo (endued)

DECREE

I receive dunamis power because the Holy Spirit fills me and is upon me. I am clothed with dunamis power from on high. I am filled to overflowing with the Holy Spirit and dunamis. For the sake of Christ and His Kingdom, I go about doing good and healing those oppressed by the enemy.

Chapter 4

THE THREE-STRAND CONDUIT

Hope, Faith, and Love

"Oh no! My engine won't start!"

I was in a hurry (as always) to make it to an appointment. I turned the key (back in the day when you actually had to insert the key and turn it manually), but the engine wouldn't turn on. My car wasn't going anywhere, which meant I was not going to make it to my appointment. The car had everything it needed to function including an engine and a full tank of gas, so what was the problem?

According to the mechanic, my fuel injectors were clogged, so the gas wasn't traveling to the engine. No gas, no go! The gas was in the tank but could not get to the engine.

You might have the Spirit of God dwelling within you, and you might have the passion in your soul and the capability in your physical body to minister the dunamis of God, but if the fuel can't get to the engine, there will be no results. No matter how much you might long for power to be released in and through your life, there will be no fulfillment of that desire. Check your fuel injectors!

In this chapter I will introduce you to a three-part conduit through which dunamis will flow in and through you: hope, faith, and love.

The Source of All Power

As we have already established, in God is all power! Everything you need is in Him, and He has given you access to His power through Jesus Christ. His power is available to you.

The Distributor of His Power

If God is the source of all power, who is the distributor of it? That would be YOU. The Earth was created by God, but it was given to mankind to steward. In Christ we have been granted authority to steward the Kingdom of God in the Earth. As His ambassadors, we represent God and have full permission and authority through Christ to manifest His will and purposes. He chose to partner with us. We are His kings, priests, ambassadors, sons, and daughters, and co-laborers with Christ. To advance His Kingdom on the Earth, we need His power.

If God is the source of power, and we are His distributors, how do we get the power to flow from Him through us? Let's look at hope, faith, and love and see how they form a three-strand conduit in the spirit for the release of His dunamis.

"A cord of three strands is not quickly broken."

–Ecclesiastes 4:12b

Hope

Hope defined is: "A feeling of expectation and desire for a certain thing to happen."[4] The key word in this definition is *expectation*—positive expectation! Whenever there is an environment of expectation, miracles are waiting to happen. If you are going to be a power broker for the Lord, it is important to always be filled with expectation for God's power to shift a situation.

An example of hope being used as a conduit for God's power to flow is found in Acts 3:1-10. These verses give an account of a man who was lame from his mother's womb and was set down every day to beg at a gate of the temple called Gate Beautiful. When he saw Peter and John headed into the temple, he asked them for alms. Peter, along with John, fixed his eyes on him and said, "Look at us." This created hope in the heart of the lame beggar.

In verse 5, the scriptures state, "And **he began to give them his attention, expecting to receive something** from them." He was hoping to receive. Expectation filled his heart. Look at what happened next:

> Then Peter said, "Silver and gold I do not have, but what I do have I give you: In the name of Jesus Christ of Nazareth, rise up and walk."
> And he took him by the right hand and lifted *him* up, and immediately his feet and ankle bones received strength.
> So he, leaping up, stood, and walked and entered the temple with them—walking, leaping, and praising God.

---

4 Definitions from Oxford Languages Online Dictionary

And all the people saw him walking and praising God. Then they knew that it was he who sat begging alms at the Beautiful Gate of the temple; and they were filled with wonder and amazement at what had happened to him.

–Acts 3:6-10

Hope (joyful expectation) causes power to flow. If you are going to be God's power broker, stir hope in every situation you find that needs a breakthrough or shift. Look for the potential in the circumstance and then expect change. If you lack hope, choose it. Cultivate it in your heart by turning your thoughts towards the possibilities in God. Hope is an important strand of the power conduit.

Faith

According to Hebrews 11:1, faith is the substance of things hoped for and the evidence of things not seen. I love this!

Faith is the substance of what you hope for (or joyfully expect). Faith is internal reality. When you are in true faith, you already have what you are hoping for before it manifests in the natural. When you "have it" by faith, it is only a matter of time before it manifests because it is the evidence of what you cannot see.

For example, the moment a baby is conceived, the mother has the child within her. Even though it is only a zygote in that moment, it is still a baby although in its smallest form. The mother is with child, but she cannot see it yet. The baby doesn't even show up on an ultrasound at that time, but she still has a baby within her. Her baby is already a reality.

Over the months that follow, the baby will continue to develop within the womb and will eventually come forth into full manifestation where the child can be touched, hugged, kissed, fed, and coddled. We celebrate birth from the time the baby comes into "manifestation," but the fact is, the baby was there for months prior—from the very moment of conception.

That is the way faith works. The moment you believe, you have the promise in the spirit. Conception has taken place. It might take time before it manifests in the natural realm, but if you are in true faith, you already have it.

Faith – The Heavenly Downloader

I have always referred to faith as my "heavenly downloader." The promises of God are settled in heaven for every believer, but many will not enjoy the promises. Why? Because they didn't download them.

In the computer world, data is stored in what is called the cloud. The way you access the data in the cloud is to download it into your personal computer and *voila*, it is now yours. This is a perfect picture of how you bring the blessings that are established in the heavens into your life on Earth. All the blessings are accessed by faith—your download button.

Hope is wonderful, but it does not inherit promises – faith does! When you are in true faith, you already have the promise. You are simply waiting for it to manifest.

Five Keys to Cultivate Faith

I have found these following keys to cultivate faith helpful.

1. Faith Hears

"Faith comes by hearing and hearing by the word of God."
–*Romans 10:17*

What is God's word concerning a situation that needs a demonstration of power?

Here's an example to clarify this point. Perhaps your experience has sent a message to your mind that you are rejected and despised, but what does God say about you? His Word says that you are His beloved child and that you have been granted favor. There is power in God's favor to demolish any assault of rejection, if you believe. Faith has no room for the lie. Faith only responds to truth. What is God saying? Is His Word speaking louder than your experiences in the natural or the assessments you have made in your mind? Faith is based on eternal truth, not on temporal facts.

Dunamis is released in partnership with the "rhema word" (Holy Spirit-quickened word) that comes to your heart. That is the word that creates faith, and when acted upon, it releases power.

Luke 1:37 in the *Amplified Bible, Classic Edition* says,

"For with God nothing is ever impossible *and* no word from God shall be without power *or* impossible of fulfillment."

In the WORD is the power, so when you hear the WORD, faith is created in you to receive and distribute the power.

One day while in prayer, I heard the Lord say that a very rebellious, unsaved person I had been praying for would receive Christ. As soon as that WORD came to me, it was finished and sealed within me. Faith was created, and I never doubted after that moment. I was not moved by what I saw outwardly because I had the WORD on it. It was my "internal reality." I rejoiced in the promise and sure enough, that person experienced the greatest miracle of all—the miracle of salvation.

Jesus said, "The words that I have spoken to you are spirit and are life." When you hear His word, faith is produced.

2. Faith Sees

Faith agrees on how God sees a situation and not on how man perceives it. We have been given spiritual eyes to see God's promises and perspectives. I love the story of God's promise to Abraham after he and Lot separated.

> "And the Lord said to Abram, after Lot had separated from him, 'Lift your eyes now and look from the place where you are—northward, southward, eastward, and westward; for all the land which you see I give to you and your descendants forever.'" –*Genesis 13:14–15*

Notice that God promised to give Abraham what he could see. To see, he had to look. This promise is for you too. "If you see it, you can have it." Allow God to show you His will and purpose concerning anything you might face.

I remember praying for a woman in a prayer line at the altar. She was barren and grieved over it. When I laid my hands on her, I saw (in my Spirit-filled imagination) her womb pregnant with a child. Immediately, faith filled me for her barrenness to be removed. I could see it! It was truly an internal reality for me. I said, "You are going to get pregnant and have a baby." The power of God hit her, and down she went, falling to the floor. In less than ten months, she held her first baby, and she had two more after that. The power of God broke the curse of barrenness, and she became fruitful. I saw it, and "If you see it, you can have it." Faith sees.

God created you in His image. He has imagination, and so do you. Your imagination was never meant to host evil images. You were given an imagination so you could "see" as God sees. Ask Him to forgive you for any vain or evil images that have filled your mind, and then invite Him to purify your imagination and fill you with His holy, faith-filled images.

Can you see yourself operating in God's dunamis power? Remember, If you see it through His perspective, you can have it.

3. Faith Speaks

Your words create or destroy (James 3:6-10). God created the universe with words (see Genesis 1). When in faith, your words create God's purposes. I love decreeing the Word of God. His Word is powerful. Faith-filled words are like missiles sent out to perform God's pleasure—they can blow up sickness, disease, poverty, lack, and oppression of any kind.

Faith-filled words are also like seeds sown that produce life and much fruit. Faith-filled words are power packs that carry

God's dunamis. Jesus healed the sick with a word. You can too. Faith-filled words deliver power.

4. Faith Receives

Jesus taught an important key about faith in Mark 11:24:

"Therefore I say to you, all things for which you pray and ask, believe that you have received them, and they shall be granted you."

When you are in faith, you already have the promise before it manifests. You are simply waiting for the manifestation. Have you received dunamis power? Is dunamis living big within you? Remember that receiving is not passive but focused and intentional. Receive dunamis, and let it grow within you!

5. Faith Acts

Faith without works is dead (James 2:17). Faith must be activated. If you believe in dunamis but never act on it, there will be no manifestation of power. Your action is what detonates the dunamis. Look for opportunities to work God's dunamis by faith. Miracles happen when there is a need. Find the need and then release dunamis. Activate your faith.

6. Faith Endures

Jesus said, "Assuredly, I say to you, if you have faith as a mustard seed, you will say to this mountain, 'Move from here to there,' and it will move; and nothing will be impossible for you." *–Matthew 17:20*

The mustard seed is a hearty seed with great endurance. Apparently, even if you plant a mustard seed deep into the ground and lay pavement on top of it, somehow and someway it will find its way through the soil and the pavement. If it can't go through it, it will go around it, but it will endure.

It also grows in unfavorable conditions such as along sandy dirt roads with very little earth. It will even grow inside garbage or contaminated areas. It will grow where other plants fail—choked out, eaten by bugs, or infested by disease. Nothing will stop it. It will endure.

Jesus said that if we have faith like the mustard seed, nothing will be impossible for us. What a promise!

Don't lose your faith if you do not see dunamis manifest right away. Remain strong in what you have already received by faith. You are simply waiting for the manifestation.

Years ago, when my husband and I were called by God to leave our secular careers and enter into fulltime mission and ministry work, the Lord taught us to live by faith with no visible means of financial support. We gave Him our big "yes" and were excited about the opportunity … until we weren't.

The warfare was brutal and the tests of faith were challenging beyond belief. We studied the promises and knew that God did not lie and would not fail. We had to endure. We already had the fullness of provision by faith but had not seen it manifest yet.

Eventually, our breakthrough came, but it did not manifest overnight. We endured the battle for five years. Once we received the breakthrough, we never battled lack again and have lived in abundance. We had the provision in the realm of the spirit (by faith) before it manifested. We simply had to endure.

Love

The third strand of the dunamis conduit is love. Love for God and love for others must be our aim and motive. Love is our primary commandment in the New Testament as all others are fulfilled in it. Jesus made this clear.

> *John 13:34 (NASB)*
>
> I am giving you a new commandment, that you love one another; just as I have loved you, that you also love one another.
>
> *Matthew 22:35-40 (NASB)*
>
> And one of them, a lawyer, asked Him a question, testing Him: "Teacher, which is the great commandment in the Law?" And He said to him, "'You shall love the Lord your God with all your heart, and with all your soul, and with all your mind.' This is the great and foremost commandment. The second is like it, 'You shall love your neighbor as yourself.' Upon these two commandments hang the whole Law and the Prophets."

The Apostle Paul was a very brilliant man and well educated, but he understood the importance of making love his greatest goal in life and ministry.

> *1 Corinthians 14:1 (AMPC)*
>
> Eagerly pursue *and* seek to acquire [this] love [make it your aim, your great quest…

In 1 Corinthians 13, we see the Apostle Paul pen great definitions of love, but what shook me the most was discovering within this chapter that if I did not have love, I had nothing, was nothing, and profited nothing. It states that if I have faith to move mountains, generously give, accurately prophesy, and have divine knowledge but do not have love, it all amounts to nothing.

> Though I speak with the tongues of men and of angels, but have not love, I have become sounding brass or a clanging cymbal. And though I have *the gift of* prophecy, and understand all mysteries and all knowledge, and though I have all faith, so that I could remove mountains, but have not love, I am nothing. And though I bestow all my goods to feed *the poor,* and though I give my body to be burned, but have not love, it profits me nothing. *–1 Corinthians 13:1-3*

"Oh Lord,
May our efforts and lives
not amount to nothing!"

Fill us with love!

Faith works through love (Galatians 5:6), which means power works through love. Love must be our motivation for ministering in dunamis power. You have an effective conduit for power to flow from God and through you. It is a three-strand conduit made of hope, faith, and love.

THE THREE-STRAND CONDUIT

"We must have a spirit of power toward the enemy, a spirit of love toward men, and a spirit of self-control toward ourselves."

- Watchman Nee

ACTIVATE

Invite the Lord to:

1. Cleanse your imagination through repentance, confession, and receiving forgiveness (1 John 1:9).

2. Fill your imagination with His Holy Spirit and His desire for you to walk in dunamis power.

3. Imagine yourself fulfilling His desires. As the Lord leads, see yourself filled with dunamis and being a conduit of hope, faith, and love.

DECREE

I decree in Jesus' name that I am a three-strand conduit for His dunamis power as I walk in hope, faith, and love. The dunamis of Christ flows mightily through me.

Chapter 5

MIRACLE-WORKING DUNAMIS

"Mama! Mama!" The desperate shout of a man's voice on the porch caught my attention. I opened the door to our missionary flat in Benin, Nigeria, and there he was—a tall, broad, young, African man with his beautiful little girl held in his arms. She couldn't have been more than four years old, but I noticed that her legs were twisted and malformed.

I invited him and his daughter to sit in our lounge area and offered them something to drink and eat, as they looked hot and weary. He explained that he had walked for miles, carrying his little girl in his arms so she could receive her miracle when I prayed for her. We had ministered in several meetings in the area, and the Lord blessed the masses with many salvations and miracles. He had heard about the miracle works of God that people were experiencing, and he was desperate for his little girl to receive healing.

In a large crusade or church gathering, you have the advantage of a worship team to lead everyone into divine focus and adoration, and there is a corporate expectation created by the faith of all present (more on this aspect of dunamis in another chapter). In this type of environment, you usually minister healing and miracles after the Word is preached. The Word creates faith in the hearer, and the Lord promises to confirm His Word with signs following (Mark 16:20). In large gatherings where faith for miracles is preached, miracles always manifest.

In our lounge that day, there was no worship team and no pulpit to preach from. There was one desperate father with expectation for his daughter's healing, a little girl who was struggling with discomfort, and me. Compassion and love filled me for this precious one and her father. I had faith that God could heal this situation, but I lacked confidence that He could do it through me.

Before crusades, I would pray for hours in the Spirit and get built up in faith. I would study the Word and meditate on it for days before going into the meeting. I was completely prepared, focused, and ready when I stood on the platform to minister. But that morning, I had not spent hours in prayer or had days of specific study in the Word. I did not "feel" faith for the healing, but when I looked into the father's eyes and gazed upon the little girl, love compelled me.

I laid hands on her little malformed and twisted legs and feet, ministered healing in Jesus' name and commanded any curse of infirmity to be broken. I did not feel any power surge, and there was no outward sign that the child had been touched by God. Her father had tears streaming down his face. She struggled to get out of his arms to stand on the floor—and stand on the floor she did! I looked in amazement because it seemed that her legs and feet were perfectly straight and normal. Then she started walking … slowly at first, and then she eventually turned back and ran into her father's arms. Her father was in tears while I stood speechless. Dunamis had entered her little body and released a powerful miracle.

Her legs and feet had been deformed and twisted since birth, yet now she was completely healed. What surprised me was there was evidence of the supernatural, but it was not spectacular. What I mean is that her legs were suddenly normal, and it made me wonder if I had seen right previously. Were they really twisted and malformed previously? Did my eyes deceive me? There were no lightnings from heaven, no audible voice of God, no angelic appearance, and no power surges that I could feel or see—nothing spectacular, and yet, it was very supernatural. As she and her father embraced each other with great joy, I knew for sure that this miracle was indeed authentic. The two of them left that day so grateful to the Lord for healing her. They both walked back home praising the Lord all the way. Dunamis had produced a very special miracle for this family.

Lessons Learned

I learned much from the Holy Spirit as I reviewed the miracle. It confirmed to me the reality of the three-strand conduit for dunamis (hope, faith, and love.) All three were present. Hope was seen in this situation with the expectation and desperation of the father. He clearly had desperate expectancy for his daughter's healing—he was willing to carry her in his arms for miles in the hot sun to get prayer for her. He was expectant. He had hope.

I also learned that every miracle is a work of grace and not of works. God heals because He is God and not because we have checked all the boxes for a miracle. Even though it is important for our growth in the Lord to seek Him with a diligent heart, to faithfully study the Word, and to sow into the ministry of miracles with our time, focus, and attention, it is not our works that produce dunamis. Faith is the key: faith in God and His promises. The father had unwavering faith.

I had compassionate love and a general faith that God was able to heal her even though I lacked confidence in my own ability to partner with God in this specific situation. I learned that it was not about my "works," but that dunamis is empowered by faith working through love.

Compassionate love was present in Jesus when He worked miracles.

"And when Jesus went out, He saw a great multitude; and He was moved with compassion for them, and healed their sick."

—Matthew 14:14

I also learned that the supernatural is not always spectacular. Sometimes a miracle has taken place, but we don't realize it due to the lack of outward, tangible dynamics.

Miracle Defined

The word miracle is defined as: **an extraordinary event manifesting divine intervention in human affairs.**[5]

Types of Miracles

1. **Miracles of Creation**

This category of miracle involves divine acts that bring things into existence that were not in existence previously. For example, in Genesis 1, we see the account of God creating the heavens and the earth. He literally called things into being that were not there previously. He created light, heavens, stars, sun, moon, galaxies, universe, oceans, plants, animals, birds, fish, and humans.

> "God ... gives life to the dead and calls those things which do not exist as though they did."
>
> —*Romans 4:17b*

God has given His people the ability to do the same. I have a friend who prayed for a man who did not have an eyeball—only an empty socket. As he prayed, the eyeball formed right in front of him, and the man saw perfectly through it. This is a creative miracle. One moment there was no eyeball, and after prayer, the eyeball formed.

---

5 www.mirriam-webster.com

Jesus prayed for a man who was born blind in John 9:1-11. If he was born blind, he needed a creative miracle.

During an outpouring of the Spirit in the 1990s, we hosted many meetings where confirmed dental miracles occurred. Gold fillings often replaced copper amalgam fillings. One night a man who had lost teeth due to a previous drug addiction had teeth form in his mouth.

My husband and I heard a testimony years ago from a missionary in Africa who pointed out from the platform a man sitting in a wheelchair in the front row. He emphatically decreed, "You sir, are going to walk tonight!"

After he declared that, he realized the man had no legs. Faith drained out of him in that moment, but faith didn't drain out of the man in the wheelchair. As the minister preached about miracles, he noticed the man in the wheelchair lift himself up with his arms and then in the course of a number of seconds, bravely let go of his chair. When he let go, legs formed. The missionary shared before-and-after photos. It was amazing to hear this testimony of God's powerful creative miracle.

2. Sustaining Miracles

When you look at the stars in the sky at night, do you sometimes wonder how they remain suspended? What about the moon? What about the sustained cycles of creation? How do the seas know not to go beyond their boundaries? This is God's sustaining power at work.

God not only brought the universe into existence; He sustains it. Hebrews describes Jesus as "sustaining all things by His powerful word" (Hebrews 1:3b). And Paul refers to Jesus as "the image of the invisible God" in whom "all things hold together" (Colossians 1:15, 17).

Sustaining miracles point to the ongoing operation of nature. God's sustaining miracles allow humanity to exist and flourish.

Have you seen people go through such challenging times that you wonder how they could possibly come out on the other side, and yet, they do? This is God's sustaining miracle dunamis at work. His power will carry you through anything you might face in life.

I love the story of the widow of Zarephath (1 Kings 17:7-16). She had no means and intended to die along with her son after she made them their last meal from the little flour and oil she had left. Through Elijah's intervention, she was granted a miracle of provision, but it wasn't for just that moment. The miracle was sustained throughout the entire drought.

3. Provisional Miracles

God is your Provider. He promises to always provide for you (Philippians 4:19). He is the God of more than enough and has called you to live an abundant life. We will be studying this aspect of miracle power in another section of the book, but the Bible is full of provisional miracle accounts.

I love the faith of Abraham when the Lord called him to sacrifice his only son, Isaac. Abraham believed that God would honor his obedience. When Isaac said to his father Abraham, "'Behold, the fire and the wood, but where is the lamb for a burnt offering?' Abraham said, **'God will provide for Himself** the lamb for a burnt offering, my son.' So they went both of them together" (Genesis 22:7–8 ESV).

Dunamis produces miracles of provision.

4. Predictive Miracles

An example of a predictive miracle in the Gospels is that of Jesus telling Peter, "Go to the sea and cast a hook and take the first fish that comes up, and when you open its mouth you will find a shekel. Take that and give it to them for me and for yourself" (Matthew 17:27).

In the Old Testament we see many examples. One is that of Elijah predicting rain following a long drought (which he had also predicted). In the natural, there was no sign of rain—not even a cloud in the sky, but Elijah believed and prayed until the miracle manifested (see 1 Kings 18:41-46).

5. Healing Miracles

A great part of Jesus' call was expressed in the ministry of healing.

> And Jesus went about all Galilee, teaching in their synagogues, preaching the gospel of the kingdom, and healing all kinds of sickness and all kinds of disease among the people. Then His fame went throughout all Syria; and they brought to Him all sick people who were afflicted with various diseases and torments, and those who were demon-possessed, epileptics, and paralytics; and He healed them. *–Matthew 4:23–24*

MIRACLE-WORKING DUNAMIS

The works Jesus did you will do also and greater works (John 14:12). As the Father sent Him, so also He sends you (John 20:21), so get prepared!

One of the best ways to build your faith to operate in healing miracles is to meditate on the miracles that Jesus ministered when He lived on the Earth. The following is a list of those healing miracles for you to study. Meditate on each one and imagine yourself doing the same. Remember, "If you see it, you can have it."

Healing the royal officer's son. John 4:46-54

Healing Peter's mother-in-law. Matthew 8:14-15

Healing lepers. Luke 5:12-15; 17:11-19

Healing the centurion's servant. Matthew 8:5-13

Healing the paralyzed man. Mark 2:1-12

Healing the withered hand. Luke 6:6-10

Healing the woman with the issue of blood. Mark 5:25-34

Healing the blind. Matthew 9:27-31; 20:29-34; Mark 8:22-26; John 9:1-11

Healing the man who was an invalid for thirty-eight years. John 5:1-8

Healing many in Gennesaret. Matthew 14:34-36

Healing the deaf man with a speech impediment. Mark 7:31-37

Healing the woman who was eighteen years infirm. Luke 13:10-13

Healing a man with dropsy. Luke 4:1-6

Healing and restoring the severed ear. Luke 22:45-54

6. Deliverance Miracles

Deliverance miracles involve God's supernatural intervention to deliver out of darkness and into light and out of bondage and oppression into freedom. This can include freedom from natural adverse circumstances, deliverance from our own carnal flesh and consequence of sin, and deliverance from demonic powers and their assignments.

> "Many are the afflictions of the righteous,
> But the Lord delivers him out of them all."
> —*Psalm 34:19*

Jesus entered a synagogue in Nazareth on the Sabbath and read from Isaiah 61, then declared that what He had just read referred to Him. The religious leaders were outraged, and ALL who were in the synagogue tried to kill Him. Look at what the Scripture says about this situation.

> So all those in the synagogue, when they heard these things, were filled with wrath, and rose up and thrust Him out of the city; and they led Him to the brow of the hill on which their city was built, that they might throw Him down over the cliff. Then passing through the midst of them, He went His way. *–Luke 4:28-30*

They ALL thrust Him out of the city, leading Him to a place where they could throw Him over a cliff, but somehow, He just walked through their midst and went His way. How did this happen? Did everyone in the crowd suddenly become blind or perhaps frozen in position? Did Jesus turn invisible and walk through the mob? The Scripture doesn't share the details on how, but we know for sure a miracle took place—a miracle of deliverance.

During the time of great persecution of the church in China, we were called to smuggle Bibles. I remember one time being stopped at the security check as they had seen my Bibles on the X-Ray.

This was not good news! I prayed, and suddenly, the guards turned aside to talk to one another, and another guard in uniform showed up out of nowhere and called me through. He handed me my bags and told me to leave. When I turned around, he was gone. Was he an angel? Perhaps. One thing is for sure—I was delivered from what could have been great trouble.

One of the mandates we were commissioned to perform when we preach the gospel is to cast out demons. Jesus engaged in this form of deliverance ministry often, and you are to do so also.

> "And these signs will follow those who believe: In My name they will **cast out demons**."
>
> *—Mark 16:15*

The following are some Gospel accounts of Jesus' ministry of deliverance for you to study:

Mark 1:21-28, Luke 4:33-37 – Delivering a man possessed by a demon in Capernaum.

Matthew 8:28-32, Mark 5:1-13, Luke 8:26-33 – Delivering the Gerasene demon-possessed man.

Matthew 9:32-33 – Delivering a mute man possessed by a demon.

Matthew 15:21-28, Mark 7:24-30 – Delivering a demon-possessed girl.

Matthew 17:14-20, Mark 9:17-29, Luke 9:37-43 – Delivering a boy possessed by a demon.

Luke 11:14-28 – Delivering a mute man possessed by a demon.

Jesus commanded us to preach the gospel and cast out demons in His name. How? Remember your three-strand conduit of hope, faith, and love that releases His dunamis. Then, just do it! He is with you.

8. Resurrection Miracles

Another dunamis miracle we see in Scripture is that of resurrection. Yes, we are called to raise the dead!

The same Spirit that raised Christ from the dead dwells within you (Romans 8:11). When Jesus attended funerals, there were rumblings in the coffins. In the Gospels, Jesus raised several persons from death. These resurrections included the daughter of Jairus shortly after death (Luke 8:49-56), the son of a widow in

Nain during his funeral procession (Luke 7:11-17), and Lazarus of Bethany, who had been buried for four days (John 11:1-44).

In the Book of Acts we find Peter raising a woman named Dorcas (also called Tabitha), and the Apostle Paul resurrected a young man named Eutychus who had fallen asleep and fell from a window to his death.

Elijah (1 Kings 17:20-22) and Elisha (2 Kings 4:32-35) both saw the dead raised. Even after Elisha died, when a dead man's body touched Elisha's bones, the dead man came back to life (2 Kings 13:21).

Jesus said, "I AM THE RESURECTION AND THE LIFE…" John 11:25. He Himself was resurrected, but the dunamis of His resurrection was not confined to Him alone. When Jesus Christ died on the cross, an earthquake struck, breaking open many graves and tombs in Jerusalem. After Jesus' resurrection from the dead, many who had been dead were raised to life and appeared to many in the city (Matthew 27:50-54). Even though it is not clear how many exactly, it seemed to be a significant number. That is "Resurrection Dunamis" at work for sure!

Resurrections are increasing in this hour. In my early years after becoming a Christian, I labored in the medical field. Two other nurses along with me were born-again and filled with the Spirit around the same time, and we were all radical believers. One was working in the delivery room when a baby was born without life. She grabbed the baby in the presence of the doctor and other medical staff and shaking it, said, "You shall live and not die."

The baby came to life. We had received no training at that time as we were not aware of any Resurrection Schools—she simply obeyed the Word. She saw in the Word that we were to heal the sick, cast out devils, cleanse lepers, and raise the dead (Matthew 10:8), so she went for it, and God honored her faith.

Since that time, I have heard of many more resurrections. Dunamis will truly bring the dead to life … through you.

9. Signs and Wonders Miracles

> "Men of Israel, hear these words: Jesus of Nazareth, a Man attested by God to you by miracles, wonders, and signs which God did through Him in your midst." –*Acts 2:22*

This category of miracles is vast and can include many manifestations. During the renewal that began in 1994, for over ten years, believers regularly witnessed diverse signs and wonders when they gathered. Gold dust fell in meetings, oil poured out of the hands and feet of believers, gemstones appeared, supernatural winds blew through crowds that gathered, fragrances supernaturally filled the room, angels appeared, shakings and tremblings took place, and numerous other manifestations of signs and wonders appeared. It was truly a glorious season in the Lord, and reports of these signs were coming from all over the world.

In the Gospels, we see Jesus turning water to wine, walking on water, calming the storm, and showing up in a room that was sealed shut. These miracles could be described as signs and wonders miracles.

Dunamis will produce wonders that cause those who see them to stand in awe of God.

Working Miracles

Miracle-working dunamis is in you. One of the nine gifts of the Holy Spirit outlined in 1 Corinthians 12:4-11 is the working of miracles (v. 10). Sometimes miracles appear right before your eyes with very little effort, but in many situations, you will "work" the miracle. We see an example of this when Jesus healed the blind man at Bethsaida. It wasn't a quick delivery of a miracle. Look at how Jesus worked the miracle:

> Then He came to Bethsaida; and they brought a blind man to Him, and begged Him to touch him. So He took the blind man by the hand and led him out of the town. And when He had spit on his eyes and put His hands on him, He asked him if he saw anything.
> And he looked up and said, "I see men like trees, walking."
> Then He put His hands on his eyes again and made him look up. And he was restored and saw everyone clearly.
>
> *–Mark 8:22-25*

1. He took the blind man by the hand and led him out of town (v. 23).

2. He spit on his eyes and put His hands on him (v. 23).

3. He asked him if he saw anything (v. 23).

4. The blind man saw "men like trees walking" – perhaps blurred vision (v. 24).

5. Jesus put His hands on his eyes again (v. 25).

6. He made him look up (v. 25).

7. He received restoration of sight and saw clearly (v. 25).

Sometimes when you believe for miracles, you will not see an immediate change after ministering to the need, or you will only see a partial improvement or sign. You might want to ask the person to whom you are ministering to share any noted change. Then ask the Holy Spirit what you should do next. Obey Him, and again ask the person if there is a change. Continue to follow the Holy Spirit as you "work" the miracle.

ACTIVATE

1. Miracles manifest where there are needs. Look for some needs that require supernatural intervention and then apply your faith.

2. Make a list of five situations that require miracle intervention and declare the release of God's dunamis over each one.

3. Ask Holy Spirit how to activate dunamis in these situations.

   Holy Spirit will usually speak to you in your thoughts or imagination. Most of the time His voice is subtle, but you can become aware of His gentle nudges the more you spend time with Him.

   He might direct you to pray, declare a Word decree, or perform an action (example: Jesus spat on a man's eyes in

Mark 8:22-25 but made mud out of spit, and applied it to blind eyes in John 9:6–7) or lay hands on an individual.

4. Obey His direction and look for the outcomes.

DECREE

I decree in Jesus' name that *Miracle Working Dunamis* dwells mightily in me, and I activate it through faith and obedience at every opportunity I have. When dunamis touches lives, they are healed, delivered, resurrected, and receive miracle intervention. Now to Him who is able to do exceedingly abundantly above all that we ask or think, according to the power that works in me, be glory and honor.

Chapter 6

VIRTUE-PRODUCING DUNAMIS

Years ago, I knew a committed member of several New Age cults. She practiced witchcraft, was addicted to alcohol, swore like a trooper, and was given to destructive rage. She was emotionally and mentally unstable and constantly filled with fear and anxiety.

One night, her life changed forever. She accepted Jesus Christ as her Savior and virtue-producing dunamis filled her, transforming her from the inside out. Some of the transformation took place over time, but there was an immediate initial shedding of soul-defiling behaviors. Within days she had left the cults, stopped drinking alcohol, and cleaned up the "sewer-mouth." Rage diminished, and she was filled with love, joy, and peace. Her emotions became stable, she was filled with godly convictions and motives, and everyone that knew her noted the drastic changes.

That woman was me. I can truly testify of the moral excellence and godly conviction that dunamis produces. My worldview, personal convictions, and behaviors changed when Christ came into my life. This transformation did not come because of human influence or persuasion, it was the supernatural work of dunamis. When the Holy Spirit entered, His dunamis produced moral excellence and godly virtue within my soul.

When you are in Christ, you are called to virtue, and His dunamis enables you to live a godly and moral life.

> "His divine **power (***dunamis***)** has given to us **all** things that *pertain* to life and **godliness,** through the knowledge of Him who called us by glory and **virtue**…" –*2 Peter 1:3*

Sometimes I observe people struggling to overcome a weakness, sin, or bondage in their lives. They say things like, "I will never smoke another cigarette again," or, "I will never over-eat again." But then, they struggle with temptation and end up smoking more than they did previously, or they binge on everything in the fridge that hosts hundreds of calories per serving.

Instead of attempting to resist the negative, be filled with the positive, and it will dissolve the negative. For example, instead of using human effort to drive out an addiction, simply invite dunamis to enter in and do its work. Dunamis will produce the fruit of self-control, it will empower you to overcome temptation, and it will blow up the bondage (dunamis is the root word of dynamite).

Dunamis produces a bondage-free soul. Do you wrestle with "flesh-eating disease," with possible symptoms of gossip, pride, lies, deception, immorality, and compromise? Dunamis can deliver you and establish purity within.

VIRTUE-PRODUCING DUNAMIS

It is tragic to see believers moving effectively and powerfully in miracle-working dunamis but lacking virtue-producing dunamis. Both are available to every believer, and both are important. Too often we see those who have great faith for supernatural manifestations of the Kingdom fail to exercise faith for virtue and moral excellence.

> "A necessary pre-cursor of any great spiritual awakening is a spirit of deep humiliation growing out of a consciousness of sin and fresh revelation of the holiness and power and glory of God."
>
> *- John R. Mott*

Moral excellence and virtuous character are extremely important, and the pursuit of these attributes must not be neglected but fully embraced. Jesus, our model and standard, was, is, and will always be morally perfect. His soul is eternally saturated in excellence and perfection.

In Matthew 5, Jesus teaches what we affectionately call "The Beatitudes." The Beatitudes outline and describe the virtuous behaviors to which believers are called. Verse after verse, the high and holy standards of godly character are outlined. At the end of the chapter, Jesus concludes with:

> "Therefore you shall be perfect,
> just as your Father in heaven is perfect."
>
> *(v. 48)*

This standard of moral excellence appears unattainable, but Jesus would not call us to this level of perfection if it were impossible. Jesus taught us that "With men this is impossible, but with God all things are possible" (Matthew 19:26).

A Woman Made Whole

Let's examine the story of the woman who was healed of a long-term infirmity. She had an issue of blood for over twelve years and had sought physicians but to no avail. She was desperate and pressed in to find Jesus.

> And a certain woman, which had an issue of blood twelve years, and had suffered many things of many physicians, and had spent all that she had, and was nothing bettered, but rather grew worse, when she had heard of Jesus, came in the press behind, and touched his garment.
>
> For she said, If I may touch but his clothes, I shall be whole. And straightway the fountain of her blood was dried up; and she felt in her body that she was healed of that plague.
>
> And Jesus, immediately knowing in himself that virtue had gone out of him, turned him about in the press, and said, Who touched my clothes?
>
> And his disciples said unto him, Thou seest the multitude thronging thee, and sayest thou, Who touched me?
>
> And he looked round about to see her that had done this thing. But the woman fearing and trembling, knowing what was done in her, came and fell down before him, and told him all the truth.

VIRTUE-PRODUCING DUNAMIS

And he said unto her, Daughter, **thy faith hath made thee whole;** go in peace, and be whole of thy plague. *–Mark 5:25-33 (KJV)*

Sometimes the root of an illness is a soul issue. The root can possibly be bitterness, unforgiveness, anxiety, fear, trauma, or the consequence of immoral and sinful choices. The woman with the issue of blood, according to the law, should not have been in public. She was so desperate and faith-filled that she pressed through the crowds until she was able to grab hold of the garment of Christ. She pulled on His garment (prayer shawl) with her faith and trust. She was determined to receive the healing she was looking for with every ounce of strength in her.

It is my opinion that her illness was possibly caused by a deterrent in her soul. She needed virtue to bring alignment, which would then bring healing.

In the story of the woman with the issue of blood, we find "virtue" leaving Jesus and entering her. The word "virtue" in this portion is the Greek word dynamis (dunamis). The woman was healed of her twelve-year infirmity immediately. Perhaps there were soul issues that were healed and replaced by the virtue-producing dunamis of Christ. When the virtue was in place, the physical manifestations ceased.

Also notice that after virtue left Him and her bleeding ceased, Jesus did not say, "be healed of thy plague," but "be **whole** of thy plague." I believe it possible that His virtue-producing dunamis brought wholeness to soul issues that were broken and out of alignment, and as a result, her physical symptoms left.

A woman whom we will call Jane had been brutally raped. As a result, her soul was damaged and overcome with fear, trauma, and bitter resolve. She suffered from fibromyalgia. The memory of the rape was painful, and she found it difficult to release her bitter anger and unforgiveness. I perceived this to be the root of the fibromyalgia. She had been to many doctors and had tried many treatments but to no avail. During ministry, the dunamis of God filled her, and the trauma in her soul vanished as she was able to forgive and let the bitter anger go. The powerful virtue of God filled her, and the symptoms of fibromyalgia left her body. She was free. Virtue-producing dunamis was at work.

Peter Emphasized Excellence of Soul

I love Peter! I relate to his passion and his eagerness to serve the Lord but also his impulsiveness. Peter's struggles are revealed to us in Scripture, and I appreciate the vulnerability and candid accounts. He denied the Lord, he often acted before he thought things through, and he made harmful and unwise choices that were outside of God's will (like cutting off the arresting officer's ear – John 18:10).

Peter understood through personal experience the waywardness of the human soul and its inclinations. Even after many failures, he continued to pursue virtue. His two epistles focus on righteous behaviors. Let's look at the sobering passage he wrote to believers in 2 Peter 1:3-10 (emphasis mine):

> His **divine power (dunamis)** has given to us all things that *pertain* to life and godliness, through the knowledge of Him who

VIRTUE-PRODUCING DUNAMIS

called us by glory and virtue, by which have been given to us exceedingly great and precious promises, that through these you may be **partakers of the divine nature,** having **escaped the corruption that is in the world through lust.**

But also for this very reason, **giving all diligence, add to your faith virtue, to virtue knowledge, to knowledge self-control, to self-control perseverance, to perseverance godliness, to godliness brotherly kindness, and to brotherly kindness love.**

For if these things are yours and abound, *you* will be neither barren nor unfruitful in the knowledge of our Lord Jesus Christ. For **he who lacks these things is shortsighted, even to blindness, and has forgotten that he was cleansed from his old sins.**

Therefore, brethren, **be even more diligent to make your call and election sure, for if you do these things you will never stumble;** for so an entrance will be supplied to you abundantly into the everlasting Kingdom of our Lord and Savior Jesus Christ.

This is a powerful call to believers, and it was written by one who had failed and fallen short. He described in verse 9 the root of falling short—that we forget the work of the Spirit who cleansed us from our sin and gave us our new nature in Christ.

Peter grew in faith for the grace and the peace of God to powerfully fill him and protect him from his carnal nature. Faith in the dunamis of God to produce virtue and excellence of soul is our key.

Good News!

You do not need to lean on your own abilities to produce a virtuous soul. That will only cause you to be driven by religious effort that produces self-righteousness. The Apostle Paul taught us to put our faith in God, "for it is God who works in you both to will and to do for *His* **good pleasure**" (Philippians 2:13).

Receiving Virtue-producing Dunamis

The way you receive virtue-producing dunamis is the same way that you receive every promise of God—through faith.

In chapter three I shared an important aspect of receiving dunamis. Let's review.

Acts 1:8 says, "You shall **receive** power…" The word "receive' is a key for unlocking and igniting the dunamis in you.

When I think of the word "receive," I sense that someone will come to me with something, and I simply receive it from them. The one who delivers the blessing does the work, and I sit back and receive. It is easy. In many ways, that is how we obtain all the blessings and promises of God. We "receive" them by faith. However, the original word in the Greek for **"receive'** in Acts 1:8 does not indicate a passive receiving but an active pursuit.

Remember that the Greek word is *lambano*, which means to take; to lay hold of; to seize; to take possession, to apprehend.

The woman with the issue of blood RECEIVED virtue-producing dunamis in this way. She "laid hold of it, seized it, took possession, and apprehended it."

VIRTUE-PRODUCING DUNAMIS

Lambano is also the Greek word translated *receive* in Mark 11:24:

> "Therefore I say to you, whatever things you ask when you pray, believe that you **receive** them, and you will have them."

With intentionality and focus, lay hold of, seize, take possession, and apprehend the virtue-producing dunamis that is available to you. Don't just wait for it to come to you—go to it and RECEIVE.

Are you thirsty for virtue-producing dunamis?

Jesus said in John 7:37–28, that if we are thirsty, to come to Him and drink. You can drink of His virtue-producing dunamis. How? By faith! Sit still in His presence and drink deeply of His dunamis. Be filled. Receive.

This following prophetic act that I often engage in might help you. When I seek a fresh infilling of Holy Spirit, I position myself before Him and imagine myself drinking in His presence with every breath. As you sit in His presence, focus on Him—His holiness, His Love, His purity, His wisdom, and His power. Enjoy meditating on His greatness, then with every breath, intentionally breathe in (drink) virtue-producing dunamis by faith. Then, by faith, breathe out anything that defiles your soul.

I believe you will enjoy that exercise. Intentionally receive (lay hold, seize, take possession, and apprehend).

Some might argue that this exercise is practiced by those who engage in New Age beliefs. First, I want to emphasize that the devil is not a creator but a copy-cat. He can only counterfeit the real thing. When you discover him engaging in something, ask the Holy Spirit to show you the authentic that the enemy is attempting to counterfeit.

The following information is an even greater confirming factor for the prophetic act I invited you to partake of.

Holy Spirit is derived from two Greek words in the New Testament. The word "Holy" is *Agios*, an adjective meaning "most holy." The word "Spirit" is *Pneuma*. One of its meanings is: "breath of nostrils or mouth."[6]

Breathe in the most Holy Spirit (breath of God) and breathe out everything that is soul-defiling. Be filled with virtue-producing dunamis.

What you receive and are filled with you can freely give. When you are filled with virtue-producing dunamis, you can minister this blessing to others just like Jesus did for the woman with the issue of blood. This is why we receive dunamis—so that we can be His witnesses and do the same works He did and greater.

ACTIVATE

1. Position yourself to receive virtue-producing dunamis by engaging in the activation shared above.

2. Pray for those you know who need God's virtue-producing dunamis in their lives. Send it to them by faith through your prayers.

---

6 *Strong's Concordance of New Testament*

DECREE

Through Jesus Christ I have been granted virtue-producing dunamis. I receive moral excellence and His powerful dunamis that enables me to walk in the nature of God. Through the Holy Spirit that rests upon me, I am empowered by virtue-producing dunamis.

Chapter 7

EXPONENTIAL DUNAMIS

Yikes! The fruit became rotten… and the penny turned into a million dollars. What?! How?

I was watching a video on YouTube that explained the word "exponential." They started with a bowl of blueberries that had some very trace amounts of bacteria. The video revealed that you could eat them "as is," and they would be sweet to taste, and there would probably be no negative effects on your body. If, however, the blueberries were not washed and sat out in a warm room too long, the bacteria would double three times every hour.

They showed on the video the infected blueberries that had been left out in a warm room, and they were creepy—disgusting for sure. The small amounts of trace bacteria had multiplied and transformed the beautiful blueberries into garbage in no time.

They then took the equation of the bacteria doubling three times in an hour and applied it to a penny.

After 1 hour – the one penny produced 8 cents (1 doubled = 2; 2 doubled = 4; 4 doubled = 8)

After 2 Hours - 64 cents

After 3 hours - $5

After 4 hours - $41

After 5 hours - $328

After 6 hours - $2612

After 7 hours - $21,000

After 8 hours - $168,000

After 9 hours - $1,300,000

After 10 hours - $10,000,000

Between 12 and 13 hours you become a BILLIONAIRE!

If that is exponential, I would like some!

The definition of *exponential* is: (of an increase) becoming more and more rapid.[7]

We see this factor revealed in Deuteronomy 32:30, "…one could chase a thousand, and two put ten thousand to flight…"

You would think that if one could chase a thousand, then two would chase two thousand, but there is exponential power at work here. One puts a thousand to flight and two, ten thousand.

One of the definitions of dunamis is: the power and resources arising from numbers. There is power and increase that comes through numbers.

Let's look at the example of the five-fold ministry gifts Paul taught on in Ephesians 4:11-13.

---

[7] Oxford Languages Online Dictionary

And He Himself gave some to be apostles, some prophets, some evangelists, and some pastors and teachers, for the equipping of the saints for the work of ministry, for the edifying of the body of Christ, till we all come to the unity of the faith and of the knowledge of the Son of God, to a perfect man, to the measure of the stature of the fullness of Christ.

If a local body of believers has only a pastor ministering to the people, the power for the believers to be fully equipped and brought into the full measure of the stature of Christ will be greatly minimized. If you add an evangelist, you will increase the dynamic, but it will still lack. However, when you have all five ministry gifts active, you have the dunamis available to resource and empower the church into the full expression of Christ.

Jesus also taught that if two or three are in agreement for something they ask in prayer, then power is released for fulfillment and He would be present. Power in numbers.

> "Again I say to you that if two of you agree on earth concerning anything that they ask, it will be done for them by My Father in heaven. For where two or three are gathered together in My name, I am there in the midst of them."
>
> *–Matthew 18:19–20*

Resources increase with numbers

In a church of one hundred faithful people, everyone has precious gifts that they can offer for Kingdom advancement in their city through their church. There will be a measure of funding for the vision of the church produced within the group and a measure of volunteer service to fulfill the church's vision. The greater the vision, the more people will be required to fulfill it. There is increase of power and resource that comes with numbers.

When dunamis is present, there is exponential increase and not just what is produced through a simple understanding of increase. We believe that 1+1= 2, but when dunamis is activated, you might discover that 1+1=10 or possibly 100 or 1,000 or 10,000.

Exponential Power in Seeds

We see this power activated in seed. A farmer can take one corn seed and plant it in rich soil. A single seed (or kernel) of corn may produce a plant which yields more than 600 kernels of corn per ear. That is increase. You will want to use some for your own consumption, so take the 600 kernels in one ear of corn and plant them. The one ear of kernels will potentially produce for you 360,000 more kernels. But if you take half of that first crop (180,000 kernels) and plant them, you will produce 108,000,000 kernels. The more you plant, the more you reap exponentially. One kernel does not produce only one more kernel when planted – it produces ears of corn that produce 600 kernels each.

This is only natural calculation, but exponential dunamis is supernatural!

> Jesus said, "Most assuredly, I say to you, unless a grain of wheat falls into the ground and dies, it remains alone; but if it dies, it produces much grain." *–John 12:24*

Jesus died on the cross, descended into hell, and was raised from the dead. As a result of surrendering His life in this way, billions are now in the Kingdom. That one seed of His surrendered life produced a massive harvest of souls—exponential dunamis.

When more people are saved and filled with the Holy Spirit, the more the world will be filled with righteousness and glory. Increase of numbers produces an increase of power and influence.

In historical revivals, we see exponential dunamis influence culture, political and social reform, moral alignment, and economy. The more people who surrendered their life to the Lord and His righteous ways, the more culture was influenced.

"Tipping points" are produced through an increase of "one" to the existing status of measure. For example, a social media post goes viral when a tipping point is produced.

Imagine a scale that is perfectly balanced with golden coins. When you add one more coin to one of the sides, it produces a tipping point that weighs down that side of the scale. This is a picture of the exponential dunamis.

Jesus understood the power of numbers when He taught that if He went to the Father, His people would perform His works and greater (John 14:12). Why? Because the same Spirit that was in Christ during His time on Earth as a man is now given to everyone who believes. The more people filled with His Spirit, the greater the works. Exponential dunamis!

If you seek greater fruit in your life, ask Holy Spirit to show you someone who can partner with you in faith. Their faith combined with yours will have greater impact.

I received an alarming report from a dear friend of mine one evening. Her husband had collapsed on the floor with no pulse. The medical team worked on him for an hour before he finally recorded a pulse again, then they took him to the hospital. I began to pray immediately, of course, but I knew that we needed the exponential dunamis that come from numbers who would stand in agreement and contend for the breakthrough. I contacted people of faith who would not question God's ability to resurrect every damaged and affected cell and organ.

When you are gathering numbers to stand in agreement, make sure they are people of faith. A number of negative and pessimistic people can release power too—the devil's power. Remember that the enemy comes to steal, kill, and destroy (John 10:10).

Evicting Doubters

When Jesus went to Jairus' house to raise his daughter from the dead, He sent everyone out of the room except those of great faith—the child's parents and His closest disciples. Let's read the account:

> Some messengers came from Jairus' house and told him, "Your daughter has died. Why bother the Teacher any longer?"
>
> Jesus paid no attention to what they said, but told him, "Don't be afraid, only believe." Then he did not let anyone else go on with him except Peter and James and his brother John. They arrived at Jairus' house, where Jesus saw the confusion and heard all the loud crying and wailing. He went

in and said to them, "Why all this confusion? Why are you crying? The child is not dead—she is only sleeping!"

They started making fun of him, so he put them all out, took the child's father and mother and his three disciples, and went into the room where the child was lying. He took her by the hand and said to her, *"Talitha, koum,"* which means, "Little girl, I tell you to get up!"

She got up at once and started walking around. (She was twelve years old.) When this happened, they were completely amazed. But Jesus gave them strict orders not to tell anyone, and he said, "Give her something to eat."

–*Mark 5:35-43*

The Exponential Dunamis of Unity

When believers are united in belief and in vision, power is released.

> Behold, how good and how pleasant it is
> For brethren to dwell together in unity!
>
> It is like the precious oil upon the head,
> Running down on the beard,
> The beard of Aaron,
> Running down on the edge of his garments.
> It is like the dew of Hermon,
> Descending upon the mountains of Zion;
> For there the Lord commanded the blessing—
> Life forevermore.
>
> –*Psalm 133*

Unity releases blessing that not only touches those who are united in agreement but all who are affected by the blessing. We see this in civil elections and board decisions. In a particular small community, the council proposed that they build a library. Until that time they did not have a real library—books were only available to students in the small country schools and at a reading room in the city hall. The council was deadlocked by the 50/50 vote results concerning the library project. Through more communication and further casting of the vision, the council finally had a majority. Fifty-three percent were pro, forty-six percent were con, and one abstained.

As a result of the fifty-three percent, the city obtained a library for the community. Not only those in unity for the vision enjoyed the benefits of the library, but the entire city had access. The library was used for small seminars, meetings, poetry readings, and exhibits. In addition, the library gave the citizens the ability to access books that accelerated their learning, provided new scopes of interest, and enlarged their world view. The entire city was influenced and took on a new look and feel. Artists and authors began to emerge out of hiddenness with this fresh focus.

Not everyone on that board was in agreement, but those who were in unity created exponential dunamis that changed the landscape and status of the city for all who lived in the area.

Choosing the right people to come into agreement

When you are looking for those who can stand with you in agreement to produce exponential dunamis, look for the following important characteristics:

1. **Passion** – they share passion for the outcome the Lord and you desire.

2. **Commitment** – when they give you their yes to stand with you, they follow through. They make their commitment before God.

3. **Unwavering Faith** – they fully believe and are willing to stand and lay hold of the promise.

One area of ministry I serve in involves coaching authors to write books that glorify the Lord. I serve alongside a team of skilled and anointed professionals. We understand that the more books that are written and distributed, the more the Word and testimony of the Lord will fill the planet. We understand that one book can change not only one life but many, who can then pass the book on to others and create exponential impact over years and decades.

The team I work with are all in complete unity for the goal to be accomplished, and we also bring our gifts to the table. Two of us are skilled in inspiration, two in the mechanics of writing, one in marketing, and then we have a team of editors, proofers, designers, and media personnel who labor together in unity for the common goal.

One of our goals is to invite as many as possible to receive the author's training. If we graduate a class of ten, there will be ten books plus others they will write following. If however, we train a class of one hundred, or a thousand, we exponentially increase the amount of books written over the years. In addition, each book gives God glory and helps the reader know Him better. You can see how the impact will spread. When the reader understands the content they read, they then share those truths through casual conversations with many others who will hear and be impacted. It becomes hard to measure the enormous impact—it is exponential.

As a result, we are filling the earth with books, truth, and testimonies that glorify God. All the team shares like passion, commitment, and faith. We produce much more together than we can produce alone.

ACTIVATE

1. Seek the Lord for an idea, project, or need where you can apply dunamis.

2. Ask the Lord to show you what the possible outcome would look like and imagine it.

3. Write out your desire and communicate clear directives, goals, and outcomes.

4. Who would benefit you in the releasing of dunamis (i.e., a prayer partner, a number of intercessors, a skilled worker(s), a communicator and marketer, etc.)? Write out a list of individuals the Lord suggests and the areas in which you need their agreement and service.

5. Ask the Lord who to approach to partner with you and make arrangements to meet.

6. Share the full vision, along with its benefits, projected outcome, and your plan of action.

7. Release your faith and action according to your vision, believing for fulfillment.

DECREE

In Jesus' name, I decree that the power of agreement is activated in my life. I look for quality individuals to join me in believing. I choose those who share my vision, who are committed and who are filled with unwavering faith. Together, in unity, we produce powerful results for the glory of God. I am anointed with favor and those who are to walk with me are attracted to me by the Spirit.

Chapter 8

WARFARE DUNAMIS

One of the definitions of dunamis is, "The power consisting in or resting upon armies, forces, hosts." This is warfare dunamis – power that brings victory and breakthrough. In life you will face many battles, for the devil is a very real enemy. He fights against and opposes all that God represents.

> "The thief does not come except to
> steal, and to kill, and to destroy.
> I have come that they may have life,
> and that they may have it more abundantly."
> *–John 10:10*

> "Be sober, be vigilant;
> because your adversary the devil walks about like
> a roaring lion,
> seeking whom he may devour."
> *–1 Peter 5:8*

If you live on planet Earth in the realm of time, you will face battles, but the Lord has promised you the victory in each one.

> "Now thanks be to God who always leads us in triumph in Christ, and through us diffuses the fragrance of His knowledge in every place."
> –2 Corinthians 2:14

Jesus has a plan to defeat the enemy's works in the Earth, and YOU are His plan. He gave His church the dominion and power (dunamis) over the devil and his works. Let's carefully read Ephesians 1:15-23 and receive a glimpse into this plan.

> Therefore I also, after I heard of your faith in the Lord Jesus and your love for all the saints, do not cease to give thanks for you, making mention of you in my prayers: that the God of our Lord Jesus Christ, the Father of glory, may give to you the spirit of wisdom and revelation in the knowledge of Him, the eyes of your understanding being enlightened; that you may know what is **the hope of His calling, what are the riches of the glory of His inheritance in the saints, and what is the exceeding greatness of His power toward us who believe, according to the working of His mighty power** which He worked in Christ when He raised Him from the dead and **seated** *Him* **at His right hand in the heavenly** *places*, **far above all principality and power and might and dominion,** and every name that is named, not only in this age but also in that which is to come.
>
> And **He put all** *things* **under His feet, and gave Him** *to be* **head over all** *things* **to the church, which is His body, the fullness of Him who fills all in all.**

In this scripture, we discover:

1. Jesus has hope in His calling—a rich and glorious inheritance in the saints (you).
2. Great and exceeding power (dunamis) is granted to those who believe according to His mighty power *(kratos – dominion, strength, force)*.
3. Jesus is seated in heavenly places at the right hand of the Father, far above all principality, power (authority), might (dunamis), and dominion.
4. All things are under His feet.
5. He is the head over all things in the church (of which you are part).
6. His church (of which you are part) is His body in the Earth, the fullness of Him who fills all in all.

Jesus' hope is that you will manifest His power and dominion against all the works of darkness. He had a purpose in coming, and that was to destroy the works of the evil one (see 1 John 3:8). You are His hope to fulfill His purpose.

Every battle you face is meant to be won. Everything that opposes you is meant to be brought down and destroyed. You have been given warfare dunamis that will enable you to win every battle over the enemy.

Paul taught that we are battling against invisible forces and not natural enemies.

> For we do not wrestle against flesh and blood, but against principalities, against powers, against the rulers of the darkness of this age, against spiritual hosts of wickedness in the

heavenly places. Therefore, take up the whole armor of God, that you may be able to withstand in the evil day, and having done all, to stand. *–Ephesians 6:12–13*

This portion reveals a few things regarding warfare.

1. Warfare is an actual wrestle.

Sometimes, a battle is not won immediately when dunamis is proclaimed. There is *"wrestling"* involved. Strong's Concordance defines the Greek root, *pale,* to mean: *"wrestling (a contest between two in which each endeavors to throw the other, and which is decided when the victor is able to hold his opponent down with his hand upon his neck)."*

When you are in a spiritual battle, the enemy is deliberately trying to throw and hold you down so you will not rise, but the victor is the one who holds his opponent down with his hand upon his neck. You are the victor.

Considering this, Psalm 18:40-42 carries a powerful promise for you in every spiritual battle:

> You have also given me the necks of my enemies,
> So that I destroyed those who hated me.
> They cried out, but there was none to save;
> Even to the LORD, but He did not answer them.
> Then I beat them as fine as the dust before the wind;
> I cast them out like dirt in the streets.

2. Our warfare is not of the natural realm.

Even though natural circumstances will reveal the presence of warfare, you are not battling flesh and blood but powers of wickedness in the invisible, unseen dimension.

As a result, natural weapons will not win the battle. The Apostle Paul taught the church that the weapons of their warfare were not of the natural realm in 2 Corinthians 10:3-6.

> For though we walk in the flesh, we do not war according to the flesh. For the weapons of our warfare are not carnal but mighty in God for pulling down strongholds, casting down arguments and every high thing that exalts itself against the knowledge of God, bringing every thought into captivity to the obedience of Christ, and being ready to punish all disobedience when your obedience is fulfilled.

We discover in this passage that the key to releasing warfare dunamis begins with our thoughts being brought into submission to truth. The truth is, you are the victor in Christ. The truth is, two-thousand years ago, Jesus won the battle you are facing today. The truth is, you are filled with warfare dunamis that conquers the enemy.

It has been my observation that when a natural challenge hits, most individuals respond with fear and a jolt of negative expectations. The responses of "Oh no," or "What if?" are immediately activated.

If these responses aren't arrested quickly and brought into submission to the truth, they may result in the loss of the battle. I look forward to the day that my immediate response to every assault of the enemy is, "Yay! Another victory! More spoils of war are on their way unto my account!" I'm not there yet, but I long to be and am heading in that direction. This is exactly what

Paul was talking about in his letter to the Corinthian church when he proposed, "casting down arguments and every high thing that exalts itself against the knowledge of God, bringing every thought into captivity to the obedience of Christ."

3. The armor is to be put on.

By faith we clothe ourselves in Christ. He is our armor. Every part of the armor that Paul mentions in the following verses refers to aspects of Christ's protection over our lives. We are to put on the armor by believing in who we are in Christ and who He is in us. Once we put on the armor, let's not take it off. [8]

> Finally, my brethren, be strong in the Lord and in the power of His might. Put on the whole armor of God, that you may be able to stand against the wiles of the devil. For we do not wrestle against flesh and blood, but against principalities, against powers, against the rulers of the darkness of this age, against spiritual *hosts* of wickedness in the heavenly *places*. Therefore take up the whole armor of God, that you may be able to withstand in the evil day, and having done all, to stand.
>
> Stand therefore, having girded your waist with truth, having put on the breastplate of righteousness, and having shod your feet with the preparation of the gospel of peace; above all, taking the shield of faith with which you will be able to quench all the fiery darts of the wicked one. And take the helmet of salvation, and the sword of the Spirit, which is the word of God. - *Ephesians 6:10-17*

---

[8] More in-depth instruction and training on how to secure the armor of God is included in the mentoring course, *Dunamis Made Simple,* available on www.patriciaking.com – Everlasting Love Academy).

Remember, you are not an ordinary earthly being, attempting to make it to heaven. You are a heavenly being living in the Earth. You can do all things through Christ who strengthens you!

4. **Stand in the evil day**.

I believe "the evil day" mentioned in Ephesians 6:13 refers to seasons of assaults. I'm sure you know what I am saying. It is when you have been hit with one blow after another. The enemy comes at you from every side, and right when you think nothing more could go wrong, yet another jolting circumstance hits your life.

Paul said not to be shaken in these seasons, but simply stand firm in Christ and on the promises of victory. He said, "When you've done all to stand, stand." You never throw in the white towel. You never surrender. You stand. In faith, you persevere.

> "For whatever is born of God overcomes the world. And this is the victory that has overcome the world—our faith. Who is he who overcomes the world, but he who believes that Jesus is the Son of God?" –*1 John 5:4–5*

There is no quitting in these battles. If you don't quit, you win!

Jesus, the Commander in Chief

Jesus is portrayed as a mighty warrior in the Scripture. He is your Commander in Chief![9] He is the Captain of the armies of heaven and He is with you and for you!

---

9 Commander in Chief defined: *the person who exercises supreme command and control over an armed force.*

> Lift up your heads, O you gates!
> And be lifted up, you everlasting doors!
> And the King of glory shall come in.
> Who is this King of glory?
> The Lord strong and mighty,
> The Lord mighty in battle.
> Lift up your heads, O you gates!
> Lift up, you everlasting doors!
> And the King of glory shall come in.
> Who is this King of glory?
> The Lord of hosts,
> He is the King of glory. *Selah*
>
> – Psalm 24:7-10

Warring Angels

In the Kingdom of Heaven we have a Commander in Chief who wins every battle—He has never experienced one defeat and He never will. He also has a massive heavenly host created for battle. Dunamis power anoints these angels to go to war on your behalf. They partner with you and are assigned to you by Jesus Himself.

It is believed that Michael is the captain of this host of warring angels. Scripture often refers to Michael as a "chief prince" of the heavenly Kingdom. The Book of Daniel mentions him multiple times: Daniel 10:13 as "Michael, one of the chief princes" and Daniel 12:1 where "Michael, the great prince," protects the people of Israel.

Michael is also mentioned explicitly in Revelation 12:7-12, where he does battle with Satan and casts him out of heaven so that he no longer has access to God as an accuser.

The fact that he is mentioned as a "chief prince" indicates that he is a ruling angel with others who are under his command. You are in good company. There are hosts of warring angels available to battle on your behalf.

The greatest way to activate angels is to decree the Word of God. Psalm 103:20 confirms this, "Bless the Lord, you His angels, who excel in strength, who do His word, heeding the voice of His word."

> "Justice and power must be brought together, so that whatever is just may be powerful, and whatever is powerful may be just."
>
> *- Blaise Pascal*

When Is Warfare Dunamis Available?

Warfare dunamis is available whenever you need it. In any situation where the enemy is attempting to bring curse instead of blessings, lack instead of abundance, death instead of life, sickness instead of health, or destruction instead of creation, warfare dunamis is waiting to be activated. Warfare dunamis is so powerful that it will blow up the enemy's strategies and his fortresses. He has nothing to protect him from God's warfare dunamis!

However, dunamis doesn't activate itself—you have the activation switch in you. The following keys will help you understand the simplicity of battling with warfare dunamis.

1. Have nothing in common with the enemy. If you have sin in your life, the devil has legal right to hold you captive in that area (Romans 6:16). The answer is to break agreement with him. If you are in a war, you must not be a double agent! Repent from sin and receive forgiveness.

> "If we confess our sins, He is faithful and just to forgive us *our* sins and to cleanse us from all unrighteousness." *–1 John 1:9*

2. Believe that no weapon or assignment formed against you will prosper. The enemy cannot prevail and neither can any of his specific assignments.

> "No weapon formed against you shall prosper…" *–Isaiah 54:17a*

King David knew about warfare. He was constantly fighting battles. Psalm 91 gives great comfort and strength:

> He who dwells in the secret place of the Most High shall abide under the shadow of the Almighty. I will say of the Lord, "He is my refuge and my fortress; My God, in Him I will trust." Surely He shall deliver you from the snare of the fowler.

3. Repent from all doubt, fear, and unbelief. There is no doubt, fear, or unbelief in the presence of faith. Faith does not function in a doubting and unbelieving heart that is plagued with fear.

James 1:5-8 explains,

> If any of you lacks wisdom, let him ask of God, who gives to all liberally and without reproach, and it will be given to him. But let him ask in faith, with no doubting, for he who doubts is like a wave of the sea driven and tossed by the wind. For let not that man suppose that he will receive anything from the Lord; *he is* a double-minded man, unstable in all his ways.

Oftentimes we tolerate and even comfort those who are doubting and given to fear. I totally understand the compassionate mercy of the Lord, but when you are in a battle, you can lose an entire company of soldiers if one doubts or trembles at a strategic moment. There is no room for compassion in that moment. Lives depend on appropriate action. Soldiers are trained to overcome intimidation and fear. They are trained to be bold, courageous, and fearless.

I believe we need more of this type of training in the Body, and we need to be much less tolerant of fear, doubt, and unbelief in our own lives. Fear, doubt, and unbelief caused an entire generation to fail to enter their land of promise. The promise was good, but their faith wasn't.

Discipline yourself to "only believe," and train yourself in a land of peace to war against doubt, unbelief, and fear, so you will be ready when you hit the big battles. Warfare dunamis is ignited by faith.

4. Don't forget your weapons. It is important to be armored in Christ, but you also have powerful weapons of warfare available to you. We will not thoroughly study all of the Weapons of Warfare in this teaching, but the following are some weapons to utilize when engaged in warfare dunamis.[10]

Praise

"Let the high praises of God *be* in their mouth, And a two-edged sword in their hand." *–Psalm 149:6*

About midnight Paul and Silas were praying and singing hymns to God, and the other prisoners were listening to them. Suddenly there was such a violent earthquake that the foundations of the prison were shaken. At once all the prison doors flew open, and everyone's chains came loose. – *Acts 16:25–26*

Prayer

Now this is the confidence that we have in Him, that if we ask anything according to His will, He hears us. *–1 John 5:14*

Be anxious for nothing, but in everything by prayer and supplication, with thanksgiving, let your requests be made known to God; and the peace of God, which surpasses all understanding, will guard your hearts and minds through Christ Jesus. *–Philippians 4:6–7*

---

[10] More in-depth instruction and training on how to utilize these weapons are included in the mentoring course, *Dunamis Made Simple*, available on www.patriciaking.com – Everlasting Love Academy).

Speaking in Tongues

For he who speaks in a tongue does not speak to men but to God, for no one understands *him;* however, in the spirit he speaks mysteries. He who speaks in a tongue edifies himself... *–1 Corinthians 14:2,4a*

Decree of the Word

You will also declare a thing, and it will be established for you; so light will shine on your ways. *–Job 22:28*

You yourselves write a decree concerning the Jews, as you please, in the king's name, and seal it with the king's signet ring; for whatever is written in the king's name and sealed with the king's signet ring no one can revoke. *–Esther 8:8*

The Blood

And they overcame him by the blood of the Lamb and by the word of their testimony, and they did not love their lives to the death. *–Revelation 12:11*

To Him who loved us and washed us from our sins in His own blood, and has made us kings and priests to His God and Father, to Him be glory and dominion forever and ever. Amen. *–Revelation 1:5b–6*

The Gifts of the Holy Spirit

There are diversities of gifts, but the same Spirit. There are differences of ministries, but the same Lord. And there are diversities of activities, but it is the same God who works all in all. But the manifestation of the Spirit is given to each one for the profit of all: for to one is given the word of wisdom through the Spirit, to another the word of knowledge through the same Spirit, to another faith by the same Spirit, to another gifts of healings by the same Spirit, to another the working of miracles, to another prophecy, to another discerning of spirits, to another different kinds of tongues, to another the interpretation of tongues. But one and the same Spirit works all these things, distributing to each one individually as He wills. *–1 Corinthians 12:4-11*

Communion

Then Jesus said to them, "Most assuredly, I say to you, unless you eat the flesh of the Son of Man and drink His blood, you have no life in you. Whoever eats My flesh and drinks My blood has eternal life, and I will raise him up at the last day. For My flesh is food indeed, and My blood is drink indeed. He who eats My flesh and drinks My blood abides in Me, and I in him. As the living Father sent Me, and I live because of the Father, so he who feeds on Me will live because of Me. This is the bread which came down from heaven—not as your fathers ate the manna, and are dead. He who eats this bread will live forever." *–John 6: 53-58*

For as often as you eat this bread and drink this cup, you proclaim the Lord's death till He comes. *–1 Corinthians 11:26*

> "Communion, the Lord's Supper, is one of the highest and most overlooked Weapons of Spiritual Warfare."
>
> *— James Goll*

Binding and Loosing

And I will give you the keys of the kingdom of heaven, and whatever you bind on earth will be bound in heaven, and whatever you loose on earth will be loosed in heaven. – *Matthew 16:19*

The Name of Jesus

Therefore God also has highly exalted Him and given Him the name which is above every name, that at the name of Jesus every knee should bow, of those in heaven, and of those on earth, and of those under the earth, and *that every tongue should confess that Jesus Christ is Lord, to the glory of God the Father.* –Philippians 2:9-11

"Then the seventy returned with joy, saying, 'Lord, even the demons are subject to us in Your name.'" – *Luke 10:17*

Fellowship

"And they continued steadfastly in the apostles' doctrine and fellowship, in the breaking of bread, and in prayers." – *Acts 2: 42*

And let us consider one another in order to stir up love and good works, not forsaking the assembling of ourselves together, as *is* the manner of some, but exhorting *one another*, and so much the more as you see the Day approaching. – *Hebrews 10:24–25*

Action

You will never win a battle if you don't fight. The church is a force to be reckoned with. Jesus said the gates of hell would not prevail against His church (Matthew 16:18). Gates are stationary. That means the church is on the move. We are to move forward to possess and occupy. Never should we cower in a corner amid the enemy's attempts to assault. No! We are not to be put in a defensive position. We activate, pursue, and conquer.

Jesus, your Commander in Chief, will direct you in battle through the leading of His Spirit. Every battle is unique and requires a unique battle strategy. Wait on Holy Spirit for the victory-defining instruction and promise, and then obey. Sounds simple? It is, but it's not always easy.

5. Stand. All battles are not won in a moment, and sometimes there are many battles to fight before you win the war. Perseverance is vital. As mentioned earlier, throwing in the towel is not an option if you are going to see the results of warfare dunamis at work. Stand in faith. Stand in your promised victory … and do not move from your position.

There is no problem too great, no demon too strong, no bondage too oppressive, or situation too overwhelming for warfare dunamis to fail. Remember God is the God of ALL power. There is nothing too difficult for Him, and that means there is nothing too difficult for you!

> "Since the days of Pentecost,
> has the whole church ever put aside
> every other work and waited upon Him
> for ten days, that the Spirit's power might
> be manifested?
> We give too much attention to method and
> machinery and resources, and too little to
> the source of power."
>
> *- Hudson Taylor*

ACTIVATE

1. Identify an area of warfare that you are currently facing. If you do not have any area yourself at this time, identify an area of warfare someone else is fighting and give your help.

2. Invite the Holy Spirit to reveal to you any area of sin that might be a landing strip for the enemy. If He reveals anything, choose to repent, confess, and ask forgiveness. Receive forgiveness and cleansing according to 1 John 1:9.

3. Invite the Spirit of God and His warfare dunamis to fill you afresh.

4. Allow Holy Spirit to show you the plan of action for securing the victory in the battle.

5. Act according to the Holy Spirit's leading.

6. Believe in your victory.

7. Rejoice.

DECREE

I am filled with warfare dunamis that creates victories in battles. Through Jesus Christ, my Commander in Chief, I win every battle and enjoy the blessing of His victorious warfare dunamis. He is a fire around me and glory in the midst of me. Angelic warriors surround me and fight with me and for me. The Lord gives me the neck of my enemies, and no weapon formed against me prevails.

Meditate on these additional scriptures:

Now I saw heaven opened, and behold, a white horse.
And He who sat on him was called Faithful and True,
and in righteousness He judges and makes war.
His eyes were like a flame of fire,
and on His head were many crowns.

He had a name written that no one knew except Himself.
He was clothed with a robe dipped in blood,
and His name is called The Word of God.
And the armies in heaven,
clothed in fine linen, white and clean,
followed Him on white horses.

Now out of His mouth goes a sharp sword,
that with it He should strike the nations.
And He Himself will rule them with a rod of iron.
He Himself treads the winepress of the fierceness
and wrath of Almighty God.
And He has on His robe and
on His thigh a name written:

KING OF KINGS AND
LORD OF LORDS.

–Revelation 19:11-16

Have mercy upon me, O God,
According to Your lovingkindness;
According to the multitude of Your tender mercies,

Blot out my transgressions.
Wash me thoroughly from my iniquity,
And cleanse me from my sin.

For I acknowledge my transgressions,
And my sin is always before me.
Against You, You only, have I sinned,
And done this evil in Your sight—
That You may be found just when You speak,
And blameless when You judge.

Behold, I was brought forth in iniquity,
And in sin my mother conceived me.
Behold, You desire truth in the inward parts,
And in the hidden part You will make me to know wisdom.

Purge me with hyssop, and I shall be clean;
Wash me, and I shall be whiter than snow.
Make me hear joy and gladness,
That the bones You have broken may rejoice.
Hide Your face from my sins,
And blot out all my iniquities.

Create in me a clean heart, O God,
And renew a steadfast spirit within me.
Do not cast me away from Your presence,
And do not take Your Holy Spirit from me.

Restore to me the joy of Your salvation,
And uphold me by Your generous Spirit.
Then I will teach transgressors Your ways,
And sinners shall be converted to You.

Deliver me from the guilt of bloodshed, O God,
The God of my salvation,
And my tongue shall sing aloud of Your righteousness.
O Lord, open my lips,
And my mouth shall show forth Your praise.

For You do not desire sacrifice, or else I would give it;
You do not delight in burnt offering.
The sacrifices of God are a broken spirit,
A broken and a contrite heart—
These, O God, You will not despise.

Do good in Your good pleasure to Zion;
Build the walls of Jerusalem.
Then You shall be pleased with the sacrifices of righteousness,
With burnt offering and whole burnt offering;
Then they shall offer bulls on Your altar.

–Psalm 51

He who dwells in the secret place of the Most High
Shall abide under the shadow of the Almighty.
I will say of the Lord, "He is my refuge and my fortress;
My God, in Him I will trust."
Surely He shall deliver you from the snare of the fowler
And from the perilous pestilence.
He shall cover you with His feathers,
And under His wings you shall take refuge;
His truth shall be your shield and buckler.
You shall not be afraid of the terror by night,
Nor of the arrow that flies by day,

DUNAMIS MADE SIMPLE

Nor of the pestilence that walks in darkness,
Nor of the destruction that lays waste at noonday.

A thousand may fall at your side,
And ten thousand at your right hand;
But it shall not come near you.

Only with your eyes shall you look,
And see the reward of the wicked.

Because you have made the Lord, who is my refuge,
Even the Most High, your dwelling place,
No evil shall befall you,
Nor shall any plague come near your dwelling;
For He shall give His angels charge over you,
To keep you in all your ways.
In their hands they shall bear you up,
Lest you dash your foot against a stone.
You shall tread upon the lion and the cobra,
The young lion and the serpent you shall trample underfoot.

"Because he has set his love upon Me,
therefore I will deliver him;
I will set him on high, because he has known My name.
He shall call upon Me, and I will answer him;
I will be with him in trouble;
I will deliver him and honor him.

With long life I will satisfy him,
And show him My salvation."

–*Psalm 91*

Chapter 9

WEALTH-CREATING DUNAMIS

Your Four Realms of Abundance!

How many realms of abundance are you regularly experiencing? Every child of God has access to four realms of abundance, but not all will receive them. Sometimes that is because they have not been made aware of what is available to them. It is like someone who inherited an estate but never received the notification. For others, it is because they do not know how to access the inheritance, and for yet others, it is because they have not made the effort to receive.

Once again, the Greek word for "receive" in the context of receiving dunamis (Acts 1:8), *lambano*, can be applied here: take, lay hold of, seize; take possession, gain, obtain, when taken to not let go, apprehend.

Using the example of unclaimed inheritance, it would be like receiving notification that your inheritance is at the bank. All you must do is go to the bank and sign the papers to have the funds transferred into your account. If you never go to the bank and make the transfer, the funds will still be allocated to you, but they are not in your account and therefore useless to you. You are aware that the inheritance is available, but you do not go to receive. No receiving—no inheritance. I don't know about you, but I would hate to leave an inheritance not transferred. I would want to go to the bank with great anticipation and RECEIVE: take, lay hold of, seize, possess, gain, obtain, apprehend, and when taken, not let go.

God wants you to know the realms of abundance you have been given in Christ and how to access and ultimately RECEIVE them. We will cover these topics in this chapter and build your faith to activate wealth-raising dunamis in and through your life. You already have it—it just needs to transfer. [11]

In John 10:10, Jesus said that He came to give you life in abundance—not life in lack. His power and presence produce abundance regardless of where you live or your social status. The promise of abundant life is for everyone who believes in Jesus, and it is promised for every area of your life.

The Lord granted me understanding about the four realms of abundance years ago. He opened the revelation from a portion of scripture in Genesis 26:12–13 (*NASB*):

> Now Isaac sowed in that land and reaped in the same year a hundred times as much. And the Lord blessed him, and the man became rich, and continued to grow richer until he became very wealthy.

---

[11] More in-depth instruction and training on how to receive the four realms of abundance is included in the mentoring course, *Dunamis Made Simple*, available on www.patriciaking.com – Everlasting Love Academy).

Realm #1. Reaping

You reap what you sow. Every seed can potentially bring forth a harvest. In this situation, Isaac reaped one hundredfold in the same year. Jesus promised increase of thirty, sixty, and one hundredfold on seed sown into good ground (Mark 4:20). In Deuteronomy 1:11 we discover a possible increase of a thousand times.

When we sow sparingly, we reap sparingly, and when we sow bountifully, we reap bountifully (2 Corinthians 9:6). The power released for the harvest is in the seed. For the power in the seed to be activated, it must be sown. A seed that sits on a shelf will produce nothing.

Sow with expectation for the seed to produce increase according to God's promises. Your life can be filled with increase in every area if you sow seed accordingly.

Realm #2. Blessing

Isaac reaped a hundredfold in the same year, which is an amazing reward, but the scripture says, "AND the Lord blessed him." In addition to reaping what he sowed, the power of blessing was put into action. I have discovered that when I intentionally sow seed in one area of my life, other areas are blessed also. Dunamis is like a frequency in the spirit. When it is released, it influences other areas around you. The dunamis in the seed produces realms of increase AND blessing. Blessings are attracted to you when this realm is established.

Realm #3. Rich

You can be blessed but not rich. I can bless you with a gift of maybe a thousand dollars, but that does not make you rich. Rich is a realm of sustained blessing. Isaac became rich and then richer as a result of the power in the seed he sowed. "Riches" pertain to your personal abundance. When you are rich, you have more than enough to meet your needs. You are full and living in abundance.

Realm #4. Wealthy

The Lord spoke to my heart years ago about the difference between being rich and being wealthy. His desire is for us to live in a realm of extreme wealth. As previously mentioned, when you are rich, you have an abundance for your own life, but your wealth pertains to your influence. It is how you use your resources to impact the world you live in.

The realm of extreme wealth is the realm the Lord wants us to live in. He is not a mediocre God – His love is extreme! When Jesus died on the cross, He sowed His life to reap a full harvest. He loves and values every soul with an intensity we can't even imagine, but He did not die to gain only one. He died with a vision that none should perish. His wealth is His great harvest of souls.

The Lord was wealthy in anointing. He read out of the book of Isaiah in Luke 4:18, declaring that the Spirit of the Lord was upon Him to bring good news and to set captives free. He not only spoke it, He did it! The sick who came to Him were healed, the demonized were delivered, the dead were raised, the lepers were cleansed. Jesus was extremely wealthy in anointing.

He was wealthy in revelation, wisdom, favor, and resource. Many uninformed people believe Jesus was poor. That is so far from the truth. Poor people don't need treasurers. Jesus had a treasurer during His three years of ministry on Earth because He had much to steward. Historically, when power visits through revival, wealth comes with it. There are always copious amounts of wealth-creating dunamis that produces revelation, transformation in people and lives, large sums of money, acquisitions of buildings, lands, vehicles, and many other spiritual blessings involved with revival.

Aimee Semple McPherson built the Angelus Temple just a few years before the Great Depression of the 1930s hit America. During the decade of the thirties, she not only sustained the building needs, but she expanded her ministry, led masses to the Lord, fed more people through her feeding programs than the city of Los Angeles, and weekly filled the building with sick people from hospitals and ministered healing. Many who were on their death beds and hopelessly sick were gloriously healed. This is extreme wealth. This wealth is not only for those like Aimee Semple McPherson, but this realm of wealth is also for you.

Isaac's Key to Receiving Four Realms of Abundance

The key to Isaac receiving four realms of abundance was found in the seed he sowed. Every believer is to enjoy the four realms of abundance that come from sowing seed. If you want to enjoy financial wealth, then sow finances. Like Aimee Semple McPherson, if you want wealth in advancing the Kingdom through soul winning and healing anointing, then sow seeds of faith by meditating on salvation and healing scriptures, decreeing the Word on salvation and healing, and praying for people to be saved and healed.

The seed carries your potential increase and will create realms of reaping, blessing, riches, and wealth in the area where seeds are sown. Whatever area in which you want to be wealthy, sow seeds in that area. There is power in the seed to produce these realms.

If you do not have seed, ask God for it. He will give you the seed to sow, and He will multiply it.

> Now He who provides seed for the sower and bread for food will provide and multiply your seed for sowing [that is, your resources] and increase the harvest of your righteousness [which shows itself in active goodness, kindness, and love]. – *2 Corinthians 9:10 (AMP)*

You Have Power to Make Wealth

Through Christ, you have been given dunamis to make wealth, create wealth, and obtain wealth: "Every spiritual blessing in the heavenly places in Christ has been granted you and all His exceeding, great, and precious, promises" (Ephesians 1:3; 2 Peter 1:2-4).

In review, one of the five meanings of dunamis is **the power and influence which belong to riches and wealth.**

When do you receive this dunamis? When the Holy Spirit comes upon you (Acts 1:8).

WEALTH-CREATING DUNAMIS

Deuteronomy 8:18 is a very potent promise for you to embrace and receive directly into your heart as though the Lord wrote it just for you!

> "But you are to remember the Lord your God, for it is He who is giving you power to make wealth, in order to confirm His covenant..."

You are given the promise of God's dunamis that creates wealth. Let the reality of that promise fill you.

We see evidence of wealth-producing dunamis in the Scriptures. The following are some biblical examples of provisional miracles that took place when dunamis was activated. The same God who provided these miracles is at work in you.

Genesis 13:2	By God's blessing, Abraham was made rich in livestock, gold and silver.
Genesis 21:19	God provided water for Ishmael and his mother in a time of great distress.
Exodus 16:35	God's people ate supernatural manna every day for forty years in the wilderness. It was freshly supplied every morning.
Exodus 16:13	God provided quail for His people in the wilderness.
Exodus 17:1-7	God provided water from a rock amid a dry desert for His people.

Deut. 8:7-10	God prepared His people to flourish in abundance when they entered their promised land.
1 Kings 17:14	The widow of Zarephath enjoyed the replenishment miracle of her flour and oil throughout the years of drought.
1 Kings 19:5-18	God sent an angel to Elijah to feed him food that gave supernatural strength.
2 Kings 2:19–20	God purified the water in a city through Elisha so that the people would flourish and not die. They enjoyed the provision of clean water and established a community as a result.
2 Kings 4:1-7	A widow about to have her house and sons taken by creditors was given a miracle of "oil production" to pay off her debt and to sustain her family.
Matthew 17:24-27	Jesus provides for Peter to pay tax through a coin in the fish's mouth.
Mark 6:31-44	Jesus feeds a multitude of 5,000 through five loaves and two fish.
Mark 8:1-9	Jesus feeds a multitude of 4,000 through seven loaves and a few fish.
John 2:1-11	Jesus provides "new wine" at a wedding.

> "Our God has boundless resources.
> The only limit is in us.
> Our asking, our thinking,
> our praying are too small.
> Our expectations are too limited."
>
> *- A. B. Simpson*

Receiving Wealth-Creating Dunamis

1. **Believe that God wants you to receive wealth-creating dunamis.**

   Many Christians are afraid to believe that God wants them to flourish. They are bound by lack, and some even think that being poor or in lack is holy. They fear that to embrace wealth is to love money (which is the root of all evil). This is not true. For sure, we are not to love money since the *love* of money IS the root of all evil. However, God desires us to receive wealth from Him and activate His promises for His glory. You will never activate wealth-creating dunamis if you do not believe it is God's desire for you. Settle this issue now. (Note: Scripture does not say that money is the root of all evil—it is the *love of it*. Many poor people think about money all the time—even more so than many who are rich.)

   The following are some powerful scriptures to support the Lord's promises to grant you needed provision, overflow, and abundance.

Hebrews 13:5 AMP

Let your character [your moral essence, your inner nature] be free from the love of money [shun greed—be financially ethical], being content with what you have; for He has said, "I will never [under any circumstances] desert you [nor give you up nor leave you without support, nor will I in any degree leave you helpless], nor will I forsake *or* let you down *or* relax My hold on you [assuredly not]!"

Deuteronomy 28:11a,12 (NASB)

And the Lord will give you more than enough prosperity… The Lord will open for you His good storehouse, the heavens, to give rain to your land in its season and to bless every work of your hand; and you will lend to many nations, but you will not borrow.

Philippians 4:19 (AMP)

And my God will liberally supply (fill until full) your every need according to His riches in glory in Christ Jesus.

Psalm 23:1-2 (MSG)

God, my shepherd! I don't need a thing. You have bedded me down in lush meadows, you find me quiet pools to drink from.

2 Corinthians 9:8 (AMP)

And God is able to make all grace [every favor and earthly blessing] come in abundance to you, so that you may always [under all circumstances, regardless of the need] have complete sufficiency in everything [being completely self-sufficient in Him], and have an abundance for every good work *and* act of charity.

John 10:10b (TPT)

I have come to give you everything in abundance, more than you expect—life in its fullness until you overflow!

Ephesians 3:20 (TPT)

Never doubt God's mighty power to work in you. He will achieve infinitely more than your greatest request, your most unbelievable dream, and exceed your wildest imagination! He will outdo them all, for his miraculous power constantly energizes you.

2. Receive by faith

Faith is your Kingdom currency. Faith takes the promise in the invisible realm and brings it into the natural. You receive personal ownership of wealth-creating dunamis through a faith transaction. By faith receive. You know the word well by now: *lambano*—take; lay hold of; seize; take possession; gain; obtain, apprehend, not let go.

Remember the prophetic activation I gave you in an earlier chapter. Reach up into the heavens, lay hold of the promise and press it into your heart saying, "It's mine –I've got it!"

Go after it and don't let go. Activate your faith.

3. Honor God

Honor God with what is in your hand now. We have a clear promise in Scripture that when we honor God with the first and the best, the heavens open and abundance is poured out.

Malachi 3:10-12

Bring all the tithes into the storehouse,
That there may be food in My house,
And try Me now in this,"
Says the LORD of hosts,
"If I will not open for you the windows of heaven
And pour out for you *such* blessing
That *there will* not *be room* enough *to receive it.*

"And I will rebuke the devourer for your sakes,
So that he will not destroy the fruit of your ground,
Nor shall the vine fail to bear fruit for you in the field,"
Says the LORD of hosts;

"And all nations will call you blessed,
For you will be a delightful land,"
Says the LORD of hosts.

Proverbs 3:9–10 (NASB)

Honor the LORD from your wealth,
And from the first of all your produce;
Then your barns will be filled with plenty,
And your vats will overflow with new wine.

Revelation 5:12

"Worthy is the Lamb who was slain
To receive power and riches and wisdom,
And strength and honor and glory and blessing!"

4. **Sow seeds that produce wealth.**

   When you sow seed, sow with intentionality, faith, and focus.

WEALTH-CREATING DUNAMIS

You would never find a farmer throwing seed randomly into the air, hoping that it gives him a harvest. No, he calculates the yield he desires and sows accordingly. He also chooses the patch in which to sow the seed. He doesn't sow his seed into poor grade soil or into some random space on his property, but into a well-prepared, allocated area.

Too often, believers sow seed without considering the field they are sowing into and without even considering an intended harvest. We need to be wise farmers.

What do you want to reap? How much do you want to reap? This will give you an idea of what to sow and how much to sow. The following promises will bring encouragement to you and will provoke you to action.

2 Corinthians 9:6-8

Now this I say, he who sows sparingly will also reap sparingly, and he who sows bountifully will also reap bountifully. Each one must do just as he has purposed in his heart, not grudgingly or under compulsion, for God loves a cheerful giver. And God is able to make all grace abound to you, so that always having all sufficiency in everything, you may have an abundance for every good deed.

Psalm 126:5-6

Those who sow in tears shall reap with joyful shouting. He who goes to and fro weeping, carrying his bag of seed, shall indeed come again with a shout of joy, bringing his sheaves with him.

Mark 4:26-29

And He was saying, "The kingdom of God is like a man who casts seed upon the soil; and he goes to bed at night and gets up by day, and the seed sprouts and grows—how, he himself does not know.

The soil produces crops by itself; first the blade, then the head, then the mature grain in the head.

But when the crop permits, he immediately puts in the sickle, because the harvest has come."

Galatians 6:7,9

Do not be deceived, God is not mocked; for whatever a man sows, this he will also reap …

Let us not lose heart in doing good, for in due time we will reap if we do not grow weary.

Isaiah 30:23

Then He will give you rain for the seed which you will sow in the ground, and bread from the yield of the ground, and it will be rich and plenteous; on that day your livestock will graze in a roomy pasture.

5. **Diligence**

Wealth-creating dunamis comes to the diligent. It is available to every believer, but we are to work the promises and steward them well. Laziness and apathy are pathways to poverty and lack.

Proverbs 6:10–11

A little sleep, a little slumber,
a little folding of the hands to rest,

and poverty will come upon you like a robber,
and want like an armed man.

Proverbs 20:4 (NLT)

Those too lazy to plow in the right season will have no food at the harvest.

Regarding stewardship, there are some rich insights Jesus shares in the parable of the talents in Matthew 25:14–29:

> For *the kingdom of heaven is* like a man traveling to a far country, who called his own servants and delivered his goods to them. And to one he gave five talents, to another two, and to another one, to each according to his own ability; and immediately he went on a journey. Then he who had received the five talents went and traded with them, and made another five talents. And likewise he who *had received* two gained two more also. But he who had received one went and dug in the ground, and hid his lord's money. After a long time the lord of those servants came and settled accounts with them.
>
> So he who had received five talents came and brought five other talents, saying, 'Lord, you delivered to me five talents; look, I have gained five more talents besides them.' His lord said to him, 'Well *done,* good and faithful servant; you were faithful over a few things, I will make you ruler over many things. Enter into the joy of your lord.' He also who had received two talents came and said, 'Lord, you delivered to me two talents; look, I have gained two more talents besides them.' His lord said to him, 'Well *done,* good and

faithful servant; you have been faithful over a few things, I will make you ruler over many things. Enter into the joy of your lord.'

Then he who had received the one talent came and said, 'Lord, I knew you to be a hard man, reaping where you have not sown, and gathering where you have not scattered seed. And I was afraid, and went and hid your talent in the ground. Look, *there* you have *what is* yours.'

But his lord answered and said to him, 'You wicked and lazy servant, you knew that I reap where I have not sown, and gather where I have not scattered seed. So you ought to have deposited my money with the bankers, and at my coming I would have received back my own with interest. So take the talent from him, and give *it* to him who has ten talents. For to everyone who has, more will be given, and he will have abundance; but from him who does not have, even what he has will be taken away.

6. **Acknowledge Holy Spirit**

Wealth-creating dunamis is in God, and He is all around you. Acts 1:8 establishes that you receive dunamis when the Holy Spirit comes upon you. He is always present. Invite Him to come upon you and fill you afresh. He comes where He is invited.

7. **Wisdom is your friend**

Wisdom will partner with you as you live out the promise of Deuteronomy 8:18. Wisdom teaches you to create wealth, steward wealth, and distribute wealth.

WEALTH-CREATING DUNAMIS

Proverbs 3:16-18 (NLT)

She offers you long life in her right hand, and riches and honor in her left. She will guide you down delightful paths; all her ways are satisfying.

The beginning of wisdom is the fear of the Lord, so when you are filled with wisdom, you will never idolize material things or transgress into the love of money or greed. Wisdom, when adhered to, will keep you safe.

How do you receive wisdom? By loving wisdom, seeking wisdom, and asking for wisdom.

Proverbs 8:17

I love those who love me, and those who seek me diligently will find me.

James 1:5

If any of you lacks wisdom, let him ask of God, who gives to all liberally and without reproach, and it will be given to him.

Wealth-creating dunamis is yours! Let's activate.

ACTIVATE

1. Identify any area concerning your inability to live in the realm of God's wealth. (i.e., unbelief, doubt, fear, greed, love of money, etc.). Write down any ungodly beliefs that come to mind. Once you have identified them, repent, receive forgiveness, and turn to the truth. Find

the scriptures that settle the issue and write them out. Meditate on them. Choose to believe them.

2. What areas of wealth would you like to experience (anointing, relationships, finance, possessions, wisdom, etc.)? Write them down and ask Holy Spirit to show you your potential in those areas when fulfilled. Journal what He shows you.

8. Meditate (ponder, imagine, reflect, dream) on living in the fulfillment of wealth-producing dunamis. Write down what you see. Possibly create a vision board using images and text to reflect the outcome and put it somewhere where you can see it often. Keep the vision before you. Remember, "If you see it, you can have it."

9. Honor God with the first and best of your increase. Write out the promises in Malachi 3:10-12 and reflect on the promises as you honor Him.

10. Sow intentionally for the increase of wealth-producing dunamis. Write in a journal the date you sowed your seed and what you sowed it for. When your seed produces results, also write that and the date of fulfillment in your journal.

11. Often, invite the Holy Spirit to come upon you afresh and saturate you with wealth-creating dunamis.

12. Take communion, remembering Christ, His sacrifice, and His benefits.

13. Worship the Lord and offer Him thanks for His promises and for granting you wealth-creating dunamis.

"Both riches and honor come from You,

And You reign over all.

In Your hand is power and might;

In Your hand it is to make great

and to give strength to all."

— *1 Chronicles 29:12*

DECREE

I remember the LORD my God, who gives me power to make wealth, in order to confirm His covenant. This wealth-creating dunamis is mine. I have it and I activate it. I am diligent to lay hold of the promises concerning God's great abundance in my life and to activate the promises. I am filled with wealth-creating dunamis.

Chapter 10

YOU and DUNAMIS

When you receive and activate dunamis in your life, everything changes. Negatives become positives, hope-lessness turns into expectation, unbelief is overpowered by faith, sorrow becomes joy, sickness is replaced by healing and health, bondage by freedom, and poverty by riches and great wealth.

These are some of the changes that dunamis will create in your life. How exciting for you!

Don't forget the purpose!

The reason we receive dunamis is not so that we can boast about the great power we possess, or the fame that the power might produce, or the blessings that could come as a result—we receive dunamis to enable us to rightly represent Jesus in the world we live in and be His witnesses!

> "But you shall receive power when the Holy Spirit has come upon you; **and you shall be witnesses to Me** in Jerusalem, and in all Judea and Samaria, and to the end of the earth."
> *–Acts 1:8*

There are needs everywhere, and just like in the days when Jesus lived on Earth, He will meet those needs today. There wasn't a day in Jesus' ministry He lacked dunamis. Like Him, you are to carry and manifest dunamis everywhere you go.

> "As you go, proclaim this message:
> 'The kingdom of heaven has come near.'
> Heal the sick, raise the dead, cleanse those who have leprosy, drive out demons.
> Freely you have received; freely give."
>
> – *Matthew 10:7-8*

We are His ambassadors. We are His kings and priests. If we are going to represent Him well, we cannot be a powerless church. You don't have to be a Christian to do good works as important as good works are. There are many individuals and benevolent agencies that are committed to doing good works, yet they do not know the Lord. We celebrate their love, compassion, and generosity, but only through the Lord will we see supernatural power invade the natural. His people carry His supernatural dunamis. His people are His "dunamis-solutionaries" for the world's problems.

Why are so few believers operating in dunamis?

"Many are called but few are chosen." –Matthew 20:16

Even though all believers are to receive and manifest dunamis, few are manifesting it.

At the time of writing this book, surveys have calculated that there are approximately 2.5 billion people world-wide who profess to be Christians. Of the 2.5 billion, only 25% of them profess to be either Pentecostal or Charismatic in their beliefs. Of those who attend Pentecostal and Charismatic churches, a very small number are active in regularly ministering the miracle power of God—perhaps as low as 10% of the 25%. Even if every member in the Spirit-believing assemblies ministered the power of God, that still only represents about 25% of Christ's church in the Earth.

The mandate of Jesus for His people was clear. He commissioned believers to preach the gospel and manifest His power.

> And He said to them, "Go into all the world and preach the gospel to every creature. He who believes and is baptized will be saved; but he who does not believe will be condemned. And these signs will follow those who believe: In My name they will cast out demons; they will speak with new tongues; they will take up serpents; and if they drink anything deadly, it will by no means hurt them; they will lay hands on the sick, and they will recover." – *Mark 16:15-18*

"With the power of God within us,
we need never fear the powers around us."

- Woodrow Kroll

Why are there so few manifesting dunamis?

The following are some possible reasons:

1. **They have not heard.**

Some believers have not read their Bibles or have not received revelation as they read of the works of Jesus being for His people to accomplish in this day. They possibly have heard no messages or testimonies of God's power activated today through His people.

2. **They are taught that the power is not available in this dispensation.**

Sadly, many denominations do not believe that the gifts and operations of the Holy Spirit are for today. Those who attend said churches are indoctrinated with false teachings that oppose the belief that believers are to be filled and empowered with dunamis to minister in Jesus' name.

3. **They feel inadequate.**

Some do not feel adequate to minister the dunamis of the Spirit. They look at their own weaknesses and frailties rather than the grace that empowers. Some believe that there are "special" anointed ministers who are the only ones God appoints to minister dunamis.

4. **Hope deferred has made the heart sick.**

Some believe in the Word and God's ability to manifest supernatural dunamis through His people, but because of disappointments, they lack hope. Their souls have been shattered. Every believer will come to the place where their faith is challenged, but we must continue to believe and move forward.

I, too, have experienced situations where my faith was shaken with deep grief. In those times, the Lord encouraged me to continue to fervently believe and to know that in the eternal dimension, everything is reconciled to truth even if full manifestation did not materialize in the natural realm when I had hoped.

Years ago, a young boy was fighting leukemia. The boy and his parents had great faith for healing. His condition worsened, and they called on us for help. We prayed, decreed, fasted, and hosted night watches as we stood faithfully on the promises. The family received deliverance ministry sessions to take care of any generational roots that might be the source. The expectation for a miracle was constantly renewed and refreshed. Every day we stood strong in the fight, and then… he passed.

We were devastated. Our hearts were sick, and it was like we had received a massive punch to the gut that knocked every ounce of hope out of us. I personally never wanted to pray for healing again. I was devastated and experienced a variety of emotions that tormented me. I had a choice to make at that time. I could continue to believe that God's Word is true, that He is righteous, powerful, and compassionate, and that one day I would understand the dynamics of what happened, or I could "cancel" the possibility of dunamis creating miracles today… at least through me. I never wanted to believe for another miracle, but I needed to get "back in the saddle."

Truth is eternal. Facts are only temporal, they are subject to time and subject to change We may experience the temptation to pull back in ministering dunamis when we do not see results. In times of testing, we must continue to press in for the breakthrough as we stand on the Word and promises of God. If the manifestation of power does not take place on this side of time, it does on the other. We must renew our hope.

If hope deferred has made your heart sick, pursue healing and deliverance for your soul. My soul was traumatized, and I needed ministry for the personal pain when the little boy with leukemia did not manifest healing. In the place of emotional vulnerability, the devil can tempt you with accusative, angry, and cynical thoughts toward God, yourself, and others. Resist those temptations and press on.

5. **Controlled spiritual environments.**

I have unfortunately heard of situations where someone is anointed and full of faith to perform miracles, but their leaders do not release them to minister. In these cases, the individuals are oppressed and kept from fulfilling their call. Miracles and other expressions of dunamis are locked up inside of them.

There are other scenarios, however, where leadership will discipline a congregant due to sinful behaviors or patterns and restrain them from ministering for a season until healthy alignment comes. In such cases, this restraint would be warranted and wise.

6. **Doubt and unbelief.**

Doubt and unbelief can target a variety of areas that affect the operation of dunamis: the Word and what it promises, God and His willingness to perform miracles today, your own capabilities in the Lord, and looking at the "mountain"—its size and appearance of being unconquerable.

Faith involves a choice to believe. Resisting doubt and unbelief also involves a choice. If we are going to see dunamis in operation, we must cast down doubt and unbelief. It is a battle, but when you prevail, you gain a realm of operative authority—not just a miracle.

Earlier in the book, I briefly mentioned when my husband and I were called into full-time ministry. The Lord required us to lay down our careers and learn to live by faith with no visible means of financial support. The Lord instructed us to not share our needs with anyone—only Him. We were excited to be invited on this journey and studied all the promises of provision in the Scripture.

It wasn't long before all our savings were depleted, and for the next number of years, we were in a ferocious fight of faith. We chose to believe God's promises and cast down every doubt and unbelieving thought that was contrary to the Word … day after day after day!

Many times, we fought with faith to simply put a meal on the table or fill the car with gas. We fought lack and poverty, and some days the situations were devastating, but we had no

"Plan B." We had given God our "yes," so we continued to move forward. The season lasted five years—five brutally challenging years. We were not complacent. We fought hard and strong with our faith. We stood on the Word and obeyed the Word, but every day we had the opportunity to cast down doubt and unbelief.

Finally, after five years of severe testing in the battle, we secured our breakthrough. I felt the power surge and shift in the spirit the very moment the breakthrough came. Within one or two weeks of that moment, everything changed. Immediately following, the Lord assigned us to plant an outreach center in Tijuana, Mexico, where we worked amongst the poorest of the poor. We fed them, built homes for them, helped to construct orphanages and medical centers, and preached the gospel everywhere with miracles manifesting daily. There was no lack. We had more than enough. We encountered supernatural wealth-creating dunamis.

I have never known lack since. For five years I battled against doubts and unbelief and stood on the Word and promises of God. The war against poverty and lack was won in 1985, and I have lived in an established realm of ever-increasing abundance since that time both in my personal and ministry life.

7. **Procrastination.**

Often, we say to ourselves, "I should do that," or "I need to do that." When I hear statements like that, I am convinced the "do" will never happen. The statement gives us permission to delay the action required to fulfill the "do."

When we read Acts 1:8, we might think, "Oh yes, that is wonderful, I would like that," and then read on. We might think we will get back to the verse to meditate on it and activate it later, but we don't.

We might think, "someday" I should get training on how to minister God's power, or "someday" I should pray for the sick. This is procrastination, and it will hinder you from fulfilling the commission to manifest dunamis.

The following scriptures will give you some insight on the dangers of procrastination.

Ecclesiastes 11:4

Whoever watches the wind will not plant; whoever looks at the clouds will not reap.

Proverbs 14:23

All hard work brings a profit, but mere talk leads only to poverty.

Luke 9:59-62

He said to another man, "Follow me." But he replied, "Lord, first let me go and bury my father."

Jesus said to him, "Let the dead bury their own dead, but you go and proclaim the kingdom of God."

Still another said, "I will follow you, Lord; but first let me go back and say goodbye to my family."

Jesus replied, "No one who puts a hand to the plow and looks back is fit for service in the kingdom of God."

Get Ready, Get Set, Go!

Dunamis is waiting to fill, empower, ignite, and propel you unto activation. Are you ready? Let's get set and then GO!

Get Ready

1. Study the subject. Faith comes by hearing the Word. (Romans 10:17)

2. Meditate on dunamis scriptures. (Psalm 1:1-3)

3. Imagine yourself doing the works of Jesus and greater works. (John 14:12)

4. Pray in tongues to edify your inner man. (1 Corinthians 14:2,4)

5. Repent from any unconfessed sin, doubt, unbelief, or wrong motives, and receive forgiveness and cleansing. (1 John 1:9)

Get Set

1. Receive a fresh infilling of the Holy Spirit and dunamis by faith. (Acts 1:8)

2. Be filled with hope, faith, and love daily. (1 Corinthians 13:13)

3. Commit to being led by the Holy Spirit. (Galatians 5:18)

4. Commit to obeying the Holy Spirit's direction. (Romans 8:14)

GO!

1. Look for people to bless with dunamis.

2. Minister dunamis.

3. Going is not an event, it is a lifestyle.

4. Share the testimonies of God's dunamis at work.

ACTIVATE

Congratulations! You have finished reading *Dunamis Made Simple*. You are a blast of power waiting for an opportunity to explode. You have possibly gained some inspiration by reading this book, and perhaps you came to understand some things you were not aware of before. This is great, but we must have a continual commitment to action if we are going to see dunamis detonated.

Let me encourage you to constantly look for opportunities to activate. If you do, you will surely grow! There is a great harvest to bring in and God is looking for those who are willing to advance His glorious Kingdom. He is looking for those who will minister His dunamis.

You have been called for such a time as this!

DECREE

In Jesus' name, I decree that I am an ambassador for Christ in the Earth. I am subject to King Jesus and live by the laws of His Kingdom. I am filled with dunamis and have access to everything I need to be a powerbroker for His glory.

About Patricia King

Patricia King is a respected apostolic and prophetic minister of the gospel. She is an accomplished itinerant speaker, author, television host, media producer, and ministry network overseer who has given her life fully to Jesus Christ and to His Kingdom's advancement in the Earth.

She is the founder of Patricia King Ministries, Women in Ministry Network and Everlasting Love Academy. She has written many books and has produced an abundance of resources on digital media. She is also a successful business owner and an inventive entrepreneur. Patricia's reputation in the Christian community is world-renowned.

To Connect:

Patricia King website: PatriciaKing.com

Women in Ministry Network: WIMNglobal.com

Facebook: Facebook.com/PatriciaKingPage

Instagram: PatriciaKingPage

YouTube: https://www.youtube.com/c/PatriciaKingPage

Patricia King Academy: EverlastingLoveAcademy.com

More Books and Resources by Patricia King

Available at PatriciaKing.com

Receive a Glorious Revelation

Discover a path of miracle replenishment and increase in everything that pertains to you – your physical strength, your love, your time, your provision, your gifts, your anointing, and anything else that flows from you to God and others.

Receive this God-given revelation through biblical examples, insights and keys, along with practical applications, personal testimonies, and decrees for activation.

Experience Financial Breakthrough

You were created to know abundance and blessing. Not only is God well able to prosper His people, but He has given us the tools to lay hold of abundance right now. Patricia opens your eyes to God's prosperity plan for you and gives you powerful Scripture-based decrees to open heaven's windows of blessing over your life.

The Word of God never returns void; it always produces fruit. Grab hold of these decrees and get your financial breakthrough!

More Books and Resources by Patricia King

Available at PatriciaKing.com

Blessed to Bless

"Lord, I want to be a benefactor!"

When Patricia King said this, the Lord responded, "I shall both make you a benefactor and send you benefactors." God wants to do this for all His people.

Blessed to Bless offers sound principles on how to experience blessing in your own life in greater measure, then take ownership of your benefactor calling to bless others.

Created to Know Abundance

You were not created for poverty or financial devastation. You were created to know abundance and blessing. Patricia shares insights from Scripture, testimonies, revelation, and biblical principles that outline how you can cooperate with God's promise for abundance and blessing.

Step out of financial struggle and enter into miraculous provision and supernatural supply!

More Books and Resources by Patricia King

Available at PatriciaKing.com

Step into the Blessing Zone

You were created to be blessed, to know the very best that God has to offer all the days of your life. If you have been living in a place of lack, hardship, or frustration, it is time to shift into the blessing zone and know the goodness of God in every area of your life!

Patricia shares divine secrets of how you can step out of simply living day-to-day and live *In the Zone!*

Decree the Word!

Decree a thing and it shall be established. Job 22:28

The Word of God is powerful and it will profoundly influence your life. It accomplishes everything that it is sent to do.

Decree Book Third Edition. Patricia King wrote this book to help believers activate the power of the Word in key areas of their lives, including health, provision, power, love, victory, wisdom, family, business, grace, rejuvenation and many others.